Thomas Cook

Programmes and Intineraries of Cook's Grand Excursions to Europe

for 1880

Thomas Cook

Programmes and Intineraries of Cook's Grand Excursions to Europe
for 1880

ISBN/EAN: 9783744788618

Printed in Europe, USA, Canada, Australia, Japan

Cover: Foto ©Andreas Hilbeck / pixelio.de

More available books at **www.hansebooks.com**

PROGRAMMES AND ITINERARIES

OF

COOK'S

GRAND EXCURSIONS TO EUROPE

FOR 1880,

VISITING ALL CHIEF POINTS OF INTEREST IN

SCOTLAND, ENGLAND, HOLLAND,

Belgium, Germany,

SWITZERLAND, ITALY, FRANCE,

Etc., Etc.,

Leaving NEW YORK by

Inman and Anchor Lines of Steamers,

ON

APRIL 29th, JULY 3d and JULY 31st, 1880.

WITH SPECIALLY ENGRAVED MAP OF EUROPE.

UNDER THE MANAGEMENT OF

→✳ THOMAS COOK & SON, ✳←

Ludgate Circus, London, and 261 Broadway, New York.

THE ONLY SUCCESSFUL CONDUCTORS OF TOURS TO ALL PARTS OF AND AROUND THE GLOBE.

(Specially appointed by H. R. H. the Prince of Wales, Passenger Agents to the Royal British Commission, Vienna, 1873 ; Philadelphia, 1876 ; Paris, 1878.)

C.A. BARATTONI, Manager of the American Business.

CONTENTS.

THE LIBRARY OF CONGRESS

Fold-out Placeholder

This fold-out is being digitized, and will be inserted at future date.

INTRODUCTORY NOTES.

———◆◆———

In placing before the American public the programmes for our

Annual Grand Excursion Parties to Europe for 1880,

we find it necessary to define our position as the **Originators and Promoters of the European Tourist and Excursion System, and the Only successful Conductors of Tours to all parts of the Globe,** as clearly as we did when we first issued our announcements in America, as far back as the year 1866, although since that date we have had the honor of conveying *many thousands* of the citizens of the United States to all the chief points of interest in various parts of the globe, and although we have the pleasure of knowing that our arrangements have given universal satisfaction, and so have insured us a very large number of living advertisers, who are constantly recommending to their friends our system of tours, still we know that there are many thousands in America who wish to travel, and who may have heard of the name of COOK, but who have little or no idea of the enormous extent of our business, the universal facilities at our command, or the soundness and stability of our financial position and undertakings.

We would, therefore, impress upon our readers that we are not "*speculators*," whose chief object is to get the greatest profit they can out of those who intrust their interests to them; but that we are a reliable and responsible firm, with a reputation at stake as important to us as the reputation of the Bank of England is to its Governors.

Some idea of the business of our firm may be gathered from the fact that during 1878 the receipts of the firm *increased* about *one million two hundred thousand dollars*, and that for the Paris Exposition we paid the French Minister of Finance for nearly *half a million* of admissions, or for about *one-thirtieth* of the total number of admissions. Our firm consists of only two members, viz., THOMAS COOK, the originator, who has retired from active work, and JOHN M. COOK, the sole managing partner, who has had over thirty years' experience of this unique and peculiar business. These two members own the whole capital employed in working this most marvelous business, which is carried on in every quarter of the globe, and we now have *twenty-six Branch Offices*, all managed by our own salaried representatives.

Therefore, all who intrust themselves to our care may do so with the assurance that we know well that it is absolutely necessary that all travelers must return home satisfied that they have received value for the money expended, to insure the reputation of our firm being maintained.

As the founders of this peculiar system, established in 1841, we are the pioneers and leaders of tourist arrangements in all parts of the world. It is well known that our firm has been successful, and therefore it is not surprising that imitators should spring up on all sides; and since the organization of "COOK'S EXCURSION PARTIES FROM AMERICA TO EUROPE," quite a number of those who first visited Europe under our arrangements have attempted to compete with us, by copying our programmes and itineraries, and putting what they call *their* programmes of *their* tours before the American public, simply as *speculators*—not being able to carry out their own arrangements—with the special object of making large profits, to pay the expenses of themselves and their families, and having a tour to Europe, out of the few passengers who intrust themselves to their care.

The misfortune is that America is such a wide field for these *speculators* that they can almost insure making up a party; and it is not until the travelers have had experience of their arrangements, and have returned from their tour, that they find out for whose benefit they have been traveling.

We issue our programmes, in which are set forth clearly and distinctly the routes of travel provided for, the time spent at each place, the hotels at which the party stops, and defining exactly what the amount charged entitles the passengers to, besides giving a large amount of general information. We do not issue what are termed by these *speculators* "preliminary programmes," which occupy pages of high-flown language, full of names of places and points of interest which cannot possibly be visited or seen in the time allowed, and which leaves the passenger completely in the dark as to the time spent in each place, the name and class of the hotels at which the party will stay, etc.; but after the deposits, and in many cases the fares, have been paid, they then issue a brief itinerary, occupying a small percentage of the space of the preliminary, or alluring pamphlet.

The programmes we issue are compiled and placed before the public as the result of many years' *personal traveling experience*, based upon what ourselves and our responsible assistants know can be carried out within the time and cost specified; and moreover, we never intrust our parties to the inexperienced guidance of men who have never been over the routes before. The conductors who travel with our parties are the recognized representatives of the firm, and are all gentlemen of education and experience, who mingle with their parties on terms of perfect equality. Their office is to act as business manager, to engage accommodations at hotels, see to the arrangement for railway carriages, look after the baggage, and to relieve the travelers generally of the thousand and one annoyances that travelers in Europe are subjected to.

We prepare all our programmes and itineraries for personally conducted parties to Europe, with a full knowledge of our responsibility, and fully recognizing the fact that every one intrusting themselves to our care, does so in the hope that from the time they leave for Europe until they return, they may have their overworked and exhausted energies so relieved, and all the senses of pleasure and enjoyment so occupied, that they may derive all the benefit possible from the free and unfettered intercourse and commingling with foreign nationalities and scenes, and that they may return to their homes with expanded minds, enlarged and ennobled ideas, and renewed constitutions, strengthened to bear the duties before them.

This pamphlet is published at this early date for the special purpose of giving information to those who contemplate visiting Europe with one of our personally conducted parties; and in the following pages we give a complete outline of our arrangements for these parties for the present year. We have arranged for

OUR ANNUAL MAY PARTY

to leave New York by the Inman Line steamer "CITY OF BRUSSELS" on April 19th, and full particulars are given on pages 9 to 20 of this pamphlet.

OUR GRAND ANNUAL EDUCATIONAL VACATION PARTY,

which is specially designed and arranged for students, teachers, and those engaged in educational work, and which has always been largely patronized by them, will leave New York by the Anchor Line steamer "DEVONIA" of July 3d. For full particulars as to this party, see pages 21 to 38 of this pamphlet.

OUR MIDSUMMER PARTY

will leave New York by the Inman Line steamer "CITY OF RICHMOND" on July 31st. For full particulars as to this party, see pages 39 to 51 of this pamphlet.

In order to show in a more comprehensive form the routes over which these parties will travel, we have had specially engraved for this pamphlet a **Map of Europe,** which shows our extensive system of tours generally, and which shows also the routes followed by our American Excursion parties.

A short description of the principal places of interest visited by these parties is also given on pages 54 to 60.

We therefore invite all persons contemplating joining either of these parties, to carefully study our programmes, and apply to our Chief American Office, 261 Broadway, New York, or any other authorized Agency, if any further information or explanation is required, before deciding upon the party they intend to join.

Although this pamphlet is published for the special object of announcing our Personally Conducted Parties for the present year, we have pleasure in impressing upon intending travelers the fact that although Personally Conducted Parties constitute an important part of our business, we wish it to be distinctly understood that they do not average more than *five per cent.* of our receipts, and that our chief business consists of supplying travelers with

Cook's International Traveling Tickets, which enable
one or more Passengers to travel by all Chief Lines
of Steamers and Railways to any part of, or
" Around the Globe," at any time, and
do not compel the holders to
travel in parties.

Intending travelers have only to send to our Chief American Office, 261 Broadway, New York, or any accredited Agency, an outline sketch of the tour they wish to take, stating the line of steamers, the route they wish to travel by, and the time to be occupied, and we will, in return, give them a correct quotation for the total fare for their proposed journeys.

For the special comfort and convenience of those who do not wish to join a publicly advertised party, and at the same time wish to travel through Europe as comfortably as possible, and relieve themselves of the worry and anxiety of traveling alone and making their own arrangements, attending to their own baggage, securing hotel accommodation, etc., we are prepared to give quotations for

PRIVATE AND FAMILY PARTIES,

for whom, under special contract, we will undertake to send a qualified conductor for any tour they may wish to take. Of course, the charge for such parties will be higher, in proportion per passenger, than the charge made for the publicly advertised parties; but the fare will be quoted on such a basis as will simply repay us the salary and expenses of the conductor for the time he is with the party. All we require is, that at least three weeks' notice be given to our New York Office of the exact date the party will arrive in England, so that we may make the necessary arrangements for a competent conductor to meet them on landing from the steamer.

Passengers traveling in the ordinary way with our INTERNATIONAL TRAVELING TICKETS will receive the free assistance of our salaried staff of representatives, who will be found at our various offices in the chief cities in Europe and the East. They will be met on landing at the steamers, and assisted in Custom House examinations, etc.

THOMAS COOK & SON,

"The World's Ticket Office,"

261 BROADWAY, NEW YORK.

January 1st, 1880.

Annual May Party.

PROGRAMME OF
COOK'S
Special Personally Conducted Party

TO

ENGLAND, FRANCE, SWITZERLAND, ITALY,

The Rhine, Belgium and Holland,

VISITING

LONDON, PARIS, TURIN, GENOA, PISA, FLORENCE, ROME,

NAPLES, POMPEII,

Sorrento, Venice, Milan, Lake of Como, the Simplon Pass, Mt. Blanc,
Geneva, Interlaken, Lucerne, Zurich, Schaffhausen, the Black
Forest, Strasbourg, Baden Baden, Heidelberg, Mayence,
the Rhine, Cologne, Brussels, Antwerp, Amsterdam, the Hague, Rotterdam, etc.

Leaving NEW YORK, APRIL 29th, 1880,

By Inman Mail Steamer "CITY OF BRUSSELS."

94 Days' Tour, $600.

UNDER THE MANAGEMENT OF

THOMAS COOK & SON,

Originators of the Tourist and Excursion System (Established 1841), and only successful Con-
ductors of Tours and Excursions to all parts of the Globe.
Specially appointed by his Royal Highness the Prince of Wales, Sole Passenger Agents to the
Royal British Commission, Vienna, 1873, Philadelphia, 1876, and Paris, 1878.

CHIEF OFFICE, LUDGATE CIRCUS, LONDON.

Chief American Office, 261 BROADWAY, NEW YORK, P. O. Box 4197.

INTRODUCTION.

We have pleasure in announcing our first personally conducted tour to Europe for the season of 1880. Favorable arrangements have been made by us with the Inman Line S. S. Co., whereby we are enabled to offer to applicants for this party a good selection of berths, and we call special attention to. the fact that only two passengers will be placed in one state-room, thus rendering the ocean voyage as pleasant and comfortable as possible. The party will sail from New York by the steamer "CITY OF BRUSSELS," 3,775 tons burden, and one of the finest steamers of the Inman fleet, Captain FREDK. WATKINS, Commander.

The programme for this party is based on the experience of past years, and, as it will be seen, it includes the choicest and most interesting routes of European travel.

As this party will be limited in number, persons contemplating joining it should make early application

THOMAS COOK & SON.

THE ROUTE.

The party will land at Liverpool and proceed through the picturesque Derbyshire district to London. After a few days in the great city the party will go to Paris, and proceed thence to Italy, leaving the beauties of Switzerland and the Rhine to be seen on the return. The season of the year selected will find each country in its loveliest condition. Visiting Italy previous to the heated term, the party will enter Switzerland at the height of the season.

The route from Paris will be by the Paris, Lyons and Mediterranean Railway to Fontainebleau, Dijon, Modane, and through the Mt. Cenis Tunnel to Turin, when after a night's rest, proceed direct to Genoa, thence to Pisa, *via* the Riviera line; from Pisa *via* Leghorn and the coast of the Mediterranean to Civita Vecchia and Rome, where five days will be given for sight-seeing, three of which will be under the guidance of Mr. Shakspere Wood, the well-known archæologist, according to programme shown on another page; from Rome to Naples, then to Pompeii and back; a steamboat trip on the Bay of Naples, to visit the orange groves of Sorrento; the ascent of Vesuvius; from Naples back to Rome, thence to Florence, for two or three days visiting the Uffizi Gallery, the Pitti Palace, etc.; then *via* Bologna to Venice, where three days will be spent. The route is then to Verona, with its Amphitheatre almost equal to the Coliseum; then to Milan, with its magnificent Cathedral; from Milan the party will make an excursion to Bellagio on Lake Como, and thence proceed by the Simplon Pass into Switzerland, combining railway, diligence and steamboat, united in such a manner as not to fatigue, and at the same time giving the Tourist the opportunity of seeing the grandest scenery on the European Continent. After passing Sierre, Martigny will be reached, where mules or carriages will be taken for the trip across the celebrated Tête Noir to Chamounix, where abundant opportunities will be given to those who wish to visit the Mer De Glace, or to make the ascent of Mt. Blanc. Thence by diligence through Sallanches to Geneva for a short halt; then to Lausanne, Fribourg, Berne, Thun and Interlaken; thence to Giessbach, to see its beautiful Waterfall, which will be illuminated while the party is there; from there over the Lake of Brienz to the town of that name, where carriages will be waiting to convey the party over the Brunig Pass of the "Bernese Oberland" to Alpnacht, there to again take steamer on the Lake of the Four Cantons to Lucerne, where the ascent of the Righi will be made to see the sunrise; from Lucerne *via* Zug to Zurich and its lovely lake: then to Schaffhausen to see the Falls of the Rhine; from thence the route will be over the Black Forest Railway, one of the greatest engineering achievements in Europe, passing Donaueschingen, the source of the Danube, to Strasbourg, visiting its Cathedral and its wonderful clock; thence to Baden Baden and Heidelberg. From Heidelberg to Wiesbaden the route will be *via* Frankfort, stopping over one train at this last place. The next day one of the magnificent saloon express steamers will be taken for the trip down the Rhine, reaching Cologne quite early enough to visit the Cathedral, the Church of St. Ursula, with the bones of the eleven thousand virgins, etc. From Cologne *via* Verviers and Liege to Brussels, visiting the battle-field of Waterloo; thence to Antwerp *via* Malines; thence through the ancient city of Dort to the Hague, crossing the longest railway bridge in the world; thence to Amsterdam, returning *via* Utrecht to Rotterdam; and thence by one of the large steamers of the Harwich or Flushing route to London.

ITINERARY.

Thursday, April 29th.—Leave New York by Steamship "City of Brussels," at 9 a. m., for Liverpool.

N. B.—We are notified by the Steamship Company that the above-named Steamer is appointed to sail on this date: but we cannot, of course, hold ourselves responsible should any change be made and another Steamer substituted. This, however, is not likely to occur.

Sunday, May 9th.—Expect to arrive at Liverpool. (*Washington Hotel.*)

Monday, May 10th.—Proceed to London by Midland Railway, going through the celebrated Derbyshire Peak district, and passing Derby, Leicester, Bedford, etc. (*Midland Grand Hotel.*)

Tuesday, May 11th.
Wednesday, May 12th.
Thursday, May 13th.
Friday, May 14th.
Saturday, May 15th.
Sunday, May 16th.

IN LONDON. Owing to the great number of places of interest in the Metropolis, and the diversity of opinions as to which places should be visited, no formal programme for sight-seeing will be prepared, but every assistance and information will be afforded to the members of the party by our staff.

Monday, May 17th.—Leave London for Paris, *via* New Haven and Dieppe, by 8 p. m. train from London Bridge Station.

Passengers who may so desire can take an afternoon train and spend a few hours at Brighton, joining the party at New Haven in the evening.

Any passenger preferring the short sea mail route via Dover and Calais, can be supplied with tickets for that route on payment of the difference of fare.

Tuesday, May 18th.—Arrive in Paris. (*Hotel Bedford.*)

Wednesday, May 19th.
Thursday, May 20th.
Friday, May 21st.

IN PARIS. Three days will be devoted to carriage drives, visiting the principal places of interest in and around the city, including an excursion to St. Cloud, Sevres, and Versailles, in accordance with the following Programme:

FIRST DAY.

New French Opera, Grand Boulevarts, Madeleine, Place de la Concorde and Obelisk of Luxor, Champs Elysées, Palace of Industry, Palace of the Elysée, Arc de Triomphe de l'Etoile, Exhibition Buildings, Ecole Militaire, Invalides and Tomb of Napoleon, Ministry of Foreign Affairs, Palace Bourbon, Pont de la Concorde, Palace of the Legion of Honor, Palace of the Council of State (ruins), Tuileries, Palais Royal.

Bibliothèque Nationale, Bourse, Rue Lafayette, Square Montholon, St. Vincent de Paul, Northern Railway Terminus, Park of the Buttes Chaumont, Cemetery of Père la Chaise, Prison de la Roquette and Place of Execution, Place de la Bastille and Column of July, Place du Chateau d'Eau, Porte St. Martin, Porte St. Denis, La Trinité.

SECOND DAY.

St. Augustin, Park Monceau, Arc de Triomphe, Bois de Boulogne, the Lakes, Grand Cascade and Race-course, view of the Citadel of Mont Valérien, Town and Park of St. Cloud, Montretout-Buzenval, Forest of Ville d'Avray, Avenue de Picardie, Versailles, the Grand Trianon and State Carriages.

PALACE, MUSEUM AND PARK OF VERSAILLES, Avenue de Paris, Viroflay, Chaville, Sèvres and its Porcelain Manufactory (exterior), Billancourt, Fortifications of Paris, Viaduct of Auteuil, Palace of the Trocadéro, Seine Embankment, Cours la Reine.

THIRD DAY.

Column Vendôme, Garden of the Tuileries, Institute of France, Mint, Pont Neuf and Statue of Henry IV., Palace of Justice, Ste. Chapelle, Tribunal of Commerce, Conciergerie, Cour de Cassation, St. Germain l'Auxerrois, Palace and Museum of the Louvre, Palais Royal.

Place du Carrousel and Triumphal Arch, Ecole des Beaux Arts, St. Germain des Prés, St. Sulpice, Palace of the Luxembourg, St. Jacques du Haut Pas, Val de Grace, Carpet Manufactory of the Gobelins, Observatory, Statue of Marshal Ney, Fountain and Gardens of the Luxembourg, Panthéon, Bibliothèque Ste. Geneviève, St. Etienne du Mont, Fontaine Cuvier, Jardin des Plantes, Orleans Railway Terminus, Halle aux Vins, Morgue, Cathedral of Notre Dame, Hôtel Dieu, Place du Chatelet, the new Avenue de l'Opéra.

Saturday, May 22d.—Leave Paris by 8 p. m. train for Turin, via Dijon, Macon and the Mont Cenis Tunnel.

Sunday, May 23d.—Arrive in Turin at 6.20 p. m. (*Hotels Trombetta* and *d'Angleterre.*)

Monday, May 24th.—IN TURIN, visiting the Royal Palace, Museums, Cathedral, squares, etc., and leaving by the noon train for Genoa. (*Hotel de la Ville.*)

Tuesday, May 25th.—IN GENOA, visiting the Cathedral, Church of the Annunziata, Palace of the Doges, Public Gardens, etc.

Wednesday, May 26th.—Leave Genoa by Riviera Railway for PISA. (*Hotel de Londres.*)

Thursday, May 27th.—The morning will be spent in viewing the Cathedral, Baptistry, Leaning Tower, Campo Santo, etc., leaving by noon train for Rome. (*Hotel Continental.*)

Friday, May 28th.
Saturday, May 29th.
Sunday, May 30th.
Monday, May 31st.
Tuesday, June 1st.

IN ROME, three days of which will be devoted to carriage excursions, under the superintendence of Mr. Shakspere Wood, the eminent archæologist, according to the following programme:

FIRST DAY.

THE PALATINE.—The Seven Hills; remains of the Walls of Romulus and Port Mugonia; remains of Temples and edifices of the early Republic; remains of houses of the Republican period; House of Tiberius Claudius Nero, with Fresco paintings.

THE PALACE OF THE CÆSARS.—Site of the House of Augustus; Palace of Tiberius; substructions of the Palace of Caligula, and Porticos built by him to the Domus Tiberiana; great suite of State rooms, built by Domitian; Lararium, Basilica, Triclinium, &c.; Intermoutium; great Stadium of Domitian; gigantic Porticos of Septimius Severus; site of Septizonium, &c., &c.

BASILICA OF CONSTANTINE.

Arch of Titus.—Bas-relief of Soldiers carrying Seven-branched Candlestick, &c.

(After Lunch.)

The Colosseum.	Temple of Fortuna Virilis.
Temple of Venus and Rome.	Ponte Rotto and View along the
Remains of Domus Transitoria of	Tiber.
Nero.	The Cloaca Maxima.
Arch of Constantine.	Theatre of Marcellus.
Meta Sudans.	The Portico of Octavia.
Temple of Vesta.	

Second Day.

The Pantheon.

The Forum Romanum.—Via Sacra; Vicus Tuscus; Clivus Capitulinus; Temples of Castor and Pollux, the Deified Julius, Saturn, Vespasian, Concord; the Basilica Julia; Honorary Monuments, the Pedestal of Domitian's Statue, Column of Phocas; Rostrum; Arch of Septimius Severus; Portico of the Deii Consentes; the Tabularium.

The Tarpeian Rock.

The Mamertine Prison.

The Fora of the Emperors Augustus, Nerva, Trajan.

(After Lunch.)

The Golden House of Nero.

Baths of Titus.

Basilica of St. Clement; the Basilica of the Twelfth Century; the now subterranean Basilica of the Fourth Century; marvelously preserved Frescoes; House of Clement; Temple of Mithras; remains of a grand edifice of the Republican period, superimposed on a portion of the wall of the Kings, beneath the subterranean Basilica.

Basilica of St. John Lateran.

The Scala Sancta.

Aqueduct of Nero.

Basilica of St. Paul, Outside the Walls.

Third Day.

Vatican Museum of Sculpture.

The Sixtine Chapel.—Michael Angelo's "Last Judgment."

Stanze and Loggie of Raphael.

Vatican Picture Gallery.—"The Transfiguration;" "Communion of St. Jerome;" "Madonna di Foligno," &c.. &c.

(After Lunch.)

Baths of Caracalla;   Porta St. Sebastiano.

Colombaria.

The Appian Way.—Tombs of Geta, Priscilla, Cecilia Metella, Seneca, the Cotta Family, &c., &c.; Tumuli of the Horatii and Curiatii; the Villa of the Quintilli; the Ustrinum; the Circus of Romulus; the Catacombs.

Wednesday, June 2d.—Leave Rome by morning train for Naples. (*Hotel de Russie.*)

Thursday, June 3d.	IN NAPLES, during which time the party will
Friday, June 4th.	visit the principal places of interest in the
Saturday, June 5th.	city and surroundings, including carriage
Sunday, June 6th.	drives to Pompeii and Vesuvius, and a steamboat excursion on the Bay of Naples to the orange groves of Sorrento.

Monday, June 7th.—Go by morning train to Rome, sleeping at Rome. (*Hotel Continental.*)

Tuesday, June 8th.—Leave by morning train for Florence *via* Torontola and Chiusi. (*Hotel d'Europe.*)

Wednesday, June 9th
Thursday, June 10th
Friday, June 11th.

IN FLORENCE, during which time visits will be made to the Tombs of the Medicis, the Cathedral and Baptistry, Church of Santa Croce (the Westminster Abbey of Italy), the Uffizi Gallery, Palaces of the Signoria and Pitti, etc., etc.

Saturday, June 12th.—Leave Florence by morning train for Venice, *via* Bologna. The Railway line between Florence and Bologna, which intersects the Tuscan Appenines, is one of the grandest in Europe. Bridges, tunnels (45 in all), and galleries are traversed in uninterrupted succession. Beautiful views are obtained of the valleys and gorges of the Appenines and of the luxuriant plains of Tuscany, "the Garden of Italy." (*Hotel Victoria.*)

Sunday, June 13th.
Monday, June 14th,
Tuesday, June 15th.

IN VENICE, during which time gondolas will be provided for visiting the most important points of interest, including the Church of St. Marc, Royal Palace, the Palace of the Doges, the Bridge of Sighs, State Prisons, the principal Churches, Museums, Art Galleries, the Islands of the Lagoons, the Lido, etc., etc.

Wednesday, June 16th.—Leave by morning train for VERONA. (*Hotel Tower of London.*) Visits will be made to the house and tomb of Juliet, Tombs of the Scaligeri, Arch of Galieno, the Cathedral, and the Arena or Roman Amphitheatre.

Thursday, June 17th.—Leave Verona for Milan, *via* Desenzano, Brescia, etc. Between Peschiera and Desenzano a view of the picturesque Lake of Garda is obtained. (*Hotel de Milan.*)

Friday, June 18th.
Saturday, June 19th.
Sunday, June 20th.

IN MILAN. Visiting the Cathedral, dedicated to Marie Nascenti, one of the finest specimens of Gothic architecture in the world. The Gallery Vittorio Emanuele or Public Arcade, which is one of the most spacious and attractive of its kind in existence. The Arch of Peace, the Brera Collection of Pictures and Statues, the Church of Santa Maria delle Grazie, containing, in the Monastery, the celebrated "Last Supper" of Leonardo da Vinci, etc.

One day of the stay at Milan will be devoted to an excursion by rail and steamer to the romantic LAKE OF COMO, visiting Bellagio and its charming surrounding villas.

Monday, June 21st.—Leave by morning train for ARONA, situated on the shores of the beautiful Lake Maggiore. (*Hotel d' Italie et Poste.*) Leaving same evening by diligence for Brieg.

Tuesday, June 22d.—Through the magnificent and historic SIMPLON PASS, arriving at Brieg at 4.10 p. m. (*Hotel de la Poste.*)

Wednesday, June 23d.—Leave Brieg by Simplon Railway for Martigny. (*Hotel Clerc.*)

Thursday, June 24th.—Go by mules or carriages over the **TETE NOIR** to Chamounix. (*Hotel d'Angleterre*.)

Friday, June 25th.—**IN THE VALLEY OF CHAMOUNIX.** The hotel here commands a magnificent view of MONT BLANC. Excursions may be made to the Montanvert, Mauvais Pass, Mer de Glace, Chapeau, Jardin, Flegere, or to the beautiful gorges of LA DIOZA.

Saturday, June 26th.—Leave by diligence through Sallanches for Geneva. (*Hotel Metropole*.) Visits may be made to the Cathedral where Calvin preached, the Russian Church, Rathhaus, Rousseau's Island, the meeting of the waters, &c.

Sunday, June 27th.—A day of rest **AT GENEVA**, situated on the banks of the romantic Lake Leman.

Monday, June 28th.—Leave Geneva by morning train for **BERNE**, stopping over a train at Fribourg, (if considered advisable by the conductor). (*Hotel Bellevue*.) A magnificent panorama of the snowy peaks of the Bernese Alps may be seen from the garden of the Hotel, or from the terrace of the Cathedral, on a fine day. The Cathedral (1421-1573) contains a celebrated organ, on which evening recitals are given. The Clock Tower, Bear Pit, Kindli-fresser, Gothic Church, Rathhaus, &c., constitute the sight-seeing of the Capital of Switzerland.

Tuesday, June 29th.—Leave Berne by morning express train for **INTER-LAKEN**, one of the most beautiful spots in Switzerland, and in full view of the Jungfrau. (*Hotel Victoria*.)

Wednesday, June 30th.—Carriages will be provided for an excursion to Grindelwald, to see the wonderful glaciers. Short and pleasant walks may be made to Heimwehfluh, Unspunnen, Beatenberg, Thurnberg, &c., most of which places afford good views of the Lakes of Thun and Brienz.

Thursday, July 1st.—Go by afternoon boat to **GIESSBACH**, spending the night there and witnessing the illumination of the celebrated Falls. (*Giessbach Hotel*.)

Friday, July 2d.—By steamer to Brienz and by carriage over the picturesque Brunig Pass to Alpnacht, passing through Lungern and Sarnen and by the Lake of that name (4½ miles long), taking steamer at Alpnacht, on the Lake of the Four Cantons, to Lucerne. (*Swan Hotel*.)

Saturday, July 3d. ⎰ **AT LUCERNE**, during which time the ascent of the
Sunday, July 4th. ⎱ Righi will be made.

At Lucerne may be visited the Lion cut in solid rock, after design by Thorwaldsen, in memory of the Swiss Guards who fell in defending Louis XVI. against the revolutionary mob in Paris, Aug. 10th, 1792. The Glacier Garden, in which are many relics of lacustrine habitations, etc., adjoins the "Lion." The Cathedral, containing one of the best organs in Switzerland, and the quaint Church-yard, are full of interest. Old Bridges and Fortifications. The Lake of Lucerne (*Vierwaldstattersee*) is full of wild and picturesque scenery, and is associated with the legend of William Tell.

Monday, July 5th.—Go by convenient train, *via* Zug, to **ZURICH.** (*Hotel Bellevue*.) This town is noted for its manufactures. Places of interest are the Hohe promenade, offering fine views, the Cathedral, Botanical Gardens, &c.

Tuesday, July 6th.—Go by morning train to Schaffhausen; thence by train or omnibus to Neuhausen to see the Falls of the Rhine. (*Hotel Schweizerhof*.)

Wednesday, July 7th.—Leave by train by Black Forest Railway via Singen, Donaueschingen, Triberg, Hornberg, Offenberg, etc. for **STRASBOURG.** (*Hotel Maison Rouge.*)

Thursday, July 8th.—Inspect the celebrated Cathedral and its wonderful clock, and thence proceed by train, *via* Kehl and Appenweir, to Baden Baden. (*Hotel Hollande.*) An agreeable carriage excursion may be made into the Black Forest at a small cost.

Friday, July 9th.—Leave by train for **HEIDELBERG,** (*Hotel d'Europe,*) one of the charming spots in Rhenish Germany. Visit the Schloss and the great Tun, the University, Cathedral, etc.

Saturday, July 10th.—Travel by train, *via* Darmstadt, to Frankfort, stopping here for a few hours, thence to Wiesbaden. (*Grand Hotel du Rhin.*)

Sunday, July 11th.—A day of rest **AT WIESBADEN.**

Monday, July 12th.—The party will be conveyed by carriages or omnibuses to Biebrich, where they will take steamer for the voyage down the Rhine to Cologne. The voyage on one of the magnificent saloon steamers, up or down the Rhine, is one of unsurpassed interest. The banks of this noble river teem with relics of by-gone feudal splendor—ruined castles, whose associations and whose legends awaken every generous feeling, as they glide by on either hand. The ·beauty and interest of the scenery are concentrated between Bingen and Bonn, for in quick succession we pass Eltville, Rudesheim and Bingen, the Maus Thurm, Rheinstein, Lorch, Bacharach, Gutenfels, Schonberg, the Lurlei, Rheinfelz, Boppart, Coblentz, with the Ehrenbreitstein, Andernach, Rheineck, Ramengen, Godesberg, the Drachenfels, Seven Mountains, reaching Cologne early in the evening. (*Hotel Hollande.*)

Tuesday, July 13th.—**IN COLOGNE.** The morning may be spent in visiting the Cathedral, one of the finest Gothic churches in the world, begun in 1248 ; was left unfinished from the beginning of the 16th century until 1816; church of St. Ursula (12th century), with the bones of 11,000 martyred Virgins; Rathhaus (13th to 16th centuries).

Leave Cologne by express train, *via* Aix la Chapelle, Verviers and Liege, for Brussels. (*Hotel de la Poste.*)

Wednesday, July 14th. ⎱ To be spent **AT BRUSSELS,** during which time the following places will be visited : The Hotel de la Ville, Wiertz Museum, the Palace of the Duke of Arenberg, Cathedral of St. Gudule, the House of Parliament; also, carriage or railway excursion to the Battle-field of Waterloo.
Thursday, July 15th. ⎰

Friday, July 16th.—Leave Brussels, *via* Malines, for **ANTWERP.** (*Hotel d'Europe.*) The remainder of the day may be spent in visiting the Cathedral, the church of St. Jacques, the church of St. Paul, the Hotel de Ville, Museum, Zoological Gardens, etc., etc.

Saturday, July 17th.—Leave by morning train for Amsterdam, stopping en route at the Hague. This is admitted to be the prettiest place in Holland. It is the seat of the Government, and contains the Museum, with the unrivalled collections of paintings, &c., including the renowned "Bull," by Paul Potter; the "School of Anatomy," by Rembrandt, &c. (*Old Bible Hotel.*)

Sunday, July 18th.—**IN AMSTERDAM.** The Palace, Museum, Harbor and Docks, Diamond Factories, &c., may be visited.

Monday, July 19th.—Proceed by morning train to **ROTTERDAM,** (*New Bath Hotel,*) and visit the Groote Kerk (Church of St. Lawrence), Boyman's Museum, the Birthplace and Statue of Erasmus, and quaint streets. Leave same evening by Harwich Steamer for London.   Baggage examined at Harwich.

Tuesday, July 20th. ⎰ **IN LONDON.** (*Midland Grand Hotel.*)
Wednesday, July 21st. ⎱ Leaving by evening express train on Wednesday for Liverpool.

Thursday, July 22d.—Leave Liverpool on Inman Line Steamer "City of Chester," for New York.

Sunday, Aug. 1st.—Due at New York.

The Price for this Tour is $600.

WHICH INCLUDES

First-class Ocean passage both ways,   20 Days.
First-class Hotel accommodation in Great Britain, 11 Days.
First-class Hotel accommodation on the Continent, 63 Days.

———

Total, 94 Days.

IT ALSO INCLUDES :

First-class railway and steamboat traveling for the entire journey; Omnibuses and Porterage between Stations and Hotels; free transportation of 60 lbs. of Baggage; gratuities to Servants; three days' carriage drives in Paris; three days' carriages in Rome, and the services of Mr. Shakspere Wood; Trip to Pompeii and Vesuvius; Steamboat trip to Sorrento; excursion from Milan to Lake Como and back; two days gondolas in Venice; Carriages to Grindelwald; Excursion to Waterloo; fees for sight-seeing, as per Conductor's Programme, services of special local guides where necessary; and also the services of the Conductor, who acts as Interpreter and Manager.

NOTE.—*The Conductor will only pay for carriages ordered by himself, and the services of the guides will be for the whole of the party.*

Hotel provision for each country to be according to the custom of the country, viz.: in Great Britain, Meat Breakfast, Table d'Hote Dinner, Tea, Bedroom, lights, service and attendance.   On the Continent: Meat Breakfast, Dinner at Table d'Hote (with or without wine as the Hotel provides), Bedrooms, lights and service.

A Deposit of Fifty Dollars

is required from each person who decides to go with this party; when the deposit is made, the name is registered, and the berths are allotted in the exact order of these deposits, the earliest depositors, of course, receiving the best berths.

Forty dollars of this deposit may be withdrawn up to April 10th after which time the whole amount is due.

How to Join the Party.

Persons desirous of joining this party should write as early as possible, enclosing draft on any bank or postal order made payable to the order of Thos. Cook & Son. We will upon a receipt of the same, return a "Deposit Receipt" and a plan of the steamer, showing the location of the berths we can offer. Should the choice of berths be left to us, we will use our best judgment in the interest of each, and advise them at once. The balance of the money can be paid any time after April 10th.

Extension of Time.

Breaks in the Journey can be made at almost any principal point, and as the return steamship tickets are good for one year, any of the members of this party can remain in Europe at their discretion. The whole amount of fare must be paid before starting, but they can receive back the value of their unused tickets and Hotel coupons, less 10 per cent., (*Swiss Traveling Tickets excepted*) at the Chief London Office, or they can be exchanged for tickets to other points, at their full value.

On the return from the Continent, if any wish to extend their tour to the English Lakes, Scotland, and Ireland, taking the steamer at Liverpool or Queenstown, quotations will be given by Messrs. Thos. Cook & Son; and if a party of 10 or more is made up for such supplementary tour, a Conductor will be sent with them, without extra charge.

A very interesting tour from London, combining the English Lakes, Melrose, Abbotsford, Edinburgh, Stirling, the Trossachs, Loch Lomond, Loch Katrine, Glasgow, Belfast, the Giant's Causeway, Dublin, and the Lakes of Killarney, thence to Queenstown to join the steamer, may be accomplished comfortably in from 10 to 12 days. Passengers who have made up their minds to make the above tour, after they have visited the Continent, can have a quotation from the New York office for the entire fare.

Other Lines of Steamers.

Any who desire to avail themselves of this Tour, and join this party, but prefer some other line of steamers, we can accommodate them, and will give them a special quotation either higher or lower, according to the line preferred. We will also, for those who have engaged steamship passage, give quotations, and book them from Liverpool, London or Paris.

Detours.

Any member of the above party will be allowed to leave the main party to visit other localities, provided early notice be given to the Conductor, so that engagements for hotel accommodations may not be violated. Hotel coupons will be supplied to those who so leave the party for the number of days they expect to be absent. Any unused coupons to be redeemed at the advertised rate.

LETTERS may be addressed to any member of the party, care of Thomas Cook & Son, Ludgate Circus, London, and such letters will be carefully forwarded to the Conductor of the party for delivery.

MONEY, LETTERS OF CREDIT AND CIRCULAR CHECKS are issued by us at current rates, in the denomination of five or ten pounds sterling each, and are payable at nearly every point on the route, or will be cashed by the Conductor as required, and in the currency of the country where the party happens to be at the time.

Cautionary Proviso.

The liability of Alpine roads and railroads in the neighborhood of mountains to damage from storms and other influences beyond human control, renders it necessary that we should announce that we cannot be responsible for detention or expenses incurred by deviation of routes occasioned by circumstances of this nature, nor for delays or deviations that may be caused through the railways being required for military purposes.

The most that Companies will do under such circumstances is to repay the value of any tickets or proportion of tickets not used for lines thus rendered impassable; and all claims in such cases must be sent in writing, accompanied by the unused tickets, within one month from the date for which such tickets were available.

BAGGAGE.—Whilst anxious to render all possible assistance to travelers in the transport, care and registration of baggage, THOS. COOK & SON cannot admit responsibility in cases of detention, stray conveyance, damage to or loss of baggage. In all cases of transference it is necessary that baggage should be identified by its owners, especially on entering and leaving hotels and railway stations; and whenever baggage is subject to customs examination, its owners should be present to answer for it.

N. B.—Great care will be taken in the registration and conveyance of the trunks or portmanteaus of the parties whilst travelling with the Conductor; but it must be distinctly understood that all small packages, such as handbags, umbrellas, travelling rugs, &c., must remain entirely under the control of the passenger.

THOS. COOK & SON,

261 Broadway, New York.

⁎COOK'S⁎
GRAND
Annual Educational Vacation Tour
TO EUROPE,
FOR 1880.

PROGRAMME AND ITINERARY
FOR THREE SECTIONS,

Including Visits to the most interesting Cities of

SCOTLAND, ENGLAND, FRANCE, HOLLAND,
BELGIUM, GERMANY,
Switzerland and Italy,

AND INCLUDING ALSO

The River Rhine, the Mountain Passes of Switzerland, the Glaciers, Mt. Blanc, the Italian Lakes, Pompeii, Vesuvius, etc.

Section I. Providing for **51 Days' Tour,** - $300
Section II.   "   " **65 Days'** " - **400**
Section III.   "   " **86 Days'** " - **500**

Designed and arranged for Teachers, Students, those engaged in Educational work, and others who can only leave home during the Summer vacation.

To Leave New York by Anchor Line Steamer "Devonia," sailing Saturday, July 3d, 1880,

UNDER THE MANAGEMENT OF

THOMAS COOK & SON,

Originators of the Tourist and Excursion System (Established 1841), and only successful Conductors of Tours and Excursions to all parts of the Globe.
Specially appointed by His Royal Highness the Prince of Wales, Sole Passenger Agents to the Royal British Commission, Vienna, 1873, Philadelphia, 1876, and Paris, 1878.

CHIEF OFFICE, LUDGATE CIRCUS, LONDON.
CHIEF AMERICAN OFFICE, 261 BROADWAY, NEW YORK, P. O. Box 4197.

INTRODUCTION.

The Annual Educational Vacation Parties established by us in 1873 are now so well known to Americans, and so well understood, that it is not necessary for us to give any elaborate or explanatory introduction to the present programme. Over 1,000 ladies and gentlemen connected with various educational movements, representing almost every State in the Union, have visited Europe under our arrangements, in connection with these Special Excursions; and we have no doubt they have reported to thousands of friends their opinions as to the manner in which Thos. Cook & Son carry out their contracts, and the advantages they have gained by traveling under our arrangements with such associated parties, composed of kindred spirits gathered together from all parts of the States, for the object of obtaining rest, relaxation and new vigor, strengthened by the knowledge and new ideas which such a party on such tours must acquire and promulgate to each other, from the various stand-points of different individuals.

We have received very flattering testimonials from many of the members of these parties, and we know that many lasting friendships have been formed on these tours by passengers who were previously strangers to each other. We also know that international travel is one of the best means of education that can be adopted, and we are every year confirmed in this view by the great number of sermons that are preached, lectures delivered, and books published by professional ladies and gentlemen in America and Europe.

We have also proof of the advantages from the fact that quite a number of gentlemen who made their first visits to Europe under our arrangements, and *whose traveling education was derived from ourselves and our assistants*, are now drawing programmes based upon our printed announcements, and are trying to organize parties on their own account. We are quite prepared to co-operate with such gentlemen, and give them all facilities for carrying out their ideas; but we are not prepared to place such gentlemen in the position of middle-men, deriving large profits by charging the passengers more than we charge them. It must therefore be understood that we will quote the lowest possible fares to secure comfort and pleasure, and so insure the Tourist to Europe the full benefits to be derived from our system.

We have learned from past experience that it is not advisable to crowd four passengers in one state-room, as was the case with the large parties of 1878. We have therefore the pleasure of announcing that in connection with this party we have entered into special arrangements with the Anchor Line Steamship Company, whereby we are enabled to offer the best rooms on the steamer sailing July 3d, and we wish it to be distinctly understood that, with the exception of a few forward rooms (where three passengers will be placed, that all the rooms in the after-part of the ship will be occupied by *two persons only*.

The steamship "Devonia" is appointed to sail on the 3d of July, 1880. She is one of the largest and finest steamers of the Anchor Line Fleet, and is upwards of 4,000 tons burthen. She is specially adapted for conveying large parties comfortably, owing to her great size, comfort and safety; and she is fitted up in a grand and luxurious style, being provided with a large dining saloon amidships, and elegant music-room with piano and cabinet organ. A large library containing standard works is to be found in the music saloon. The staterooms are provided with all modern improvements and are well lighted and ventilated, and the table and attendance are first-class.

With these remarks, the itineraries of the three sections constituting this party are respectfully submitted, by

THOMAS COOK & SON.

THE FIRST SECTION PROVIDES

FOR VISITING

SCOTLAND, ENGLAND, HOLLAND, THE RHINE DISTRICT, BELGIUM AND FRANCE,

AND INCLUDES

Glasgow, Loch Lomond, Loch Katrine, The Trossachs,

STIRLING CASTLE,

EDINBURGH, MELROSE, ABBOTSFORD, LONDON, ROTTERDAM, THE HAGUE,

Amsterdam, Cologne, the Rhine, Wiesbaden,

BRUSSELS, PARIS, ROUEN, DIEPPE AND BRIGHTON.

51 Days from New York, back to New York, including all necessary expenses.

Fare, $300.

Itinerary of the First Section.

Saturday, July 3d.—Leave New York by Anchor Line steamer "Devonia," for Glasgow.

N. B.— We are notified by the Steamship Company that the above named Steamer is appointed to sail on this date; but, we cannot, of course, hold ourselves responsible should any change be made and another Steamer substituted. This, however, is not likely to occur.

Tuesday, July 13th.—Expect to reach Glasgow. (*Cockburn Hotel.*)

Wednesday, July 14th.—Go by early morning train to Balloch, and take steamer on Loch Lomond for Inversnaid, passing Inch Cailliach, Inch Murrin, and Inch Lonaig. Then be conveyed in coaches to Stronachlacher, and by steamer over Loch Katrine to the Trossachs, past Rob Roy's cave and Ellen's Isle. Coach will be then taken past Loch Achray and Coilantogle Ford to Callander, thence by rail to Stirling, visiting the Royal Castle, etc., and continuing the journey past the Field of Bannockburn and Linlithgow Castle to Edinburgh. (*Cockburn Hotel.*)

Thursday, July 15th.—IN EDINBURGH, visiting Holyrood Palace and Chapel, Edinburgh Castle, the Scott Monument, Calton Hill, and the other attractions of Edinburgh.

Friday, July 16th.—Leave by early train, *via* the North British Railway, for Melrose. Carriages will be taken for a visit to the ruined Abbey, and for a five-mile drive to ABBOTSFORD, the home of Sir Walter Scott; then back to Melrose Station, when train will be taken for Carlisle; then by Midland Railway through Leeds, Sheffield, Leicester, Bedford, to London. (*Midland Grand Hotel.*)

Saturday, July 17th.
Sunday, July 18th.
Monday, July 19th.
Tuesday, July 20th.
Wednesday, July 21st.

IN LONDON. Owing to the great number of places of interest in the metropolis, and the diversity of opinions as to which places should be visited, no formal programme for sight-seeing will be prepared, but every assistance and information will be afforded to the members of the party by our staff.

Thursday, July 22d.—Leave London by Harwich or Flushing route, at 8.35 p. m., for Rotterdam.

Friday, July 23d.—Arrive at ROTTERDAM, (*New Bath Hotel,*) and visit the Groote Kerk, Church of St. Lawrence, Boyman's Museum, the birthplace and Statue of Erasmus, quaint streets, &c.

Saturday, July 24th.—Leave by morning train for Amsterdam, stopping en route at the Hague. (*Old Bible Hotel.*)

Sunday, July 25th.—A day of rest AT AMSTERDAM, the Palace, Museum, Harbor and Docks, Diamond Factories, &c., may be visited.

Monday, July 26th.—Leave by morning train, *via* Utrecht and Dusseldorf, for COLOGNE. (*Hotel Hollande.*) The afternoon may be spent in visiting the Cathedral, one of the finest Gothic Churches in the world, begun in 1248, was left unfinished from the beginning of the 16th century until 1816; church of St. Ursula (12th century), with the bones of 11,000 martyred virgins; Rathaus (13th to 16th centuries), &c.

Tuesday, July 27th.—Leave Cologne by express steamer for Biebrich, Wiesbaden. The voyage on one of the magnificent steamers up or down the Rhine is one of unsurpassed interest. The banks of this noble river teem with relics of by-gone feudal splendor; ruined castles, whose associations and whose legends awaken every generous feeling as they glide by on either hand. The beauty and interest of the Rhine scenery are concentrated between Bonn and Bingen, for in quick succession we pass the Seven Mountains, the Drachenfels, Godesberg, Remagen, Rheineck, Andernach, Coblentz, with Ehrenbreitstein, Boppart, Reinfelz, the Lurlei, Schonberg, Gutenfels, Bacharach, Lorch, Rheinstein, and the Maus Thurm. After passing Bingen, Rudesheim and Eltville, the party will land at Biebrich, and proceed by omnibuses or carriages to Wiesbaden. (*Hotel du Rhin.*)

Wednesday, July 28th.—IN WIESBADEN, one of the most famous and attractive watering places in Germany.

Thursday, July 29th.—Leave by omnibuses or carriages for Biebrich, and there take steamer for Cologne. (*Hotel d'Hollande.*)

Friday, July 30th.—Leave Cologne by express train, *via* Aix la Chapelle, Verviers and Liege, for Brussels. (*Hotel de la Poste.*)

Saturday, July 31st. } **IN BRUSSELS,** during which time the following places will be visited: The Hotel de Ville, Wiertz Museum, the Palace of the Duke of Arenberg, the Cathedral of St. Gudule, the House of Parliament, etc.
Sunday, Aug. 1st. }

Monday, Aug. 2d.—Leave Brussels by morning train, *via* Mons, for Paris. (*Hotels London and New York* and *St. Petersburg.*)

Tuesday, Aug. 3d.
Wednesday, Aug. 4th.
Thursday, Aug. 5th.
Friday, Aug. 6th.
Saturday, Aug. 7th.
Sunday, Aug. 8th.
} **IN PARIS,** three days of which will be devoted to carriage drives, visiting the principal places of interest in and around the city, including an excursion to St. Cloud, Sevres and Versailles, in accordance with the following programme:

FIRST DAY.

New French Opera, Grand Boulevarts, Madeleine, Place de la Concorde and Obelisk of Luxor, Champs Elysées, Palace of Industry, Palace of the Elysée, Arc de Triomphe de l'Etoile, Exhibition Buildings, Ecole Militaire, Invalides and Tomb of Napoleon, Ministry of Foreign Affairs, Palace Bourbon, Pont de la Concorde, Palace of the Legion of Honor, Palace of the Council of State (ruins), Tuileries, Palais Royal.

Bibliothèque Nationale, Bourse, Rue Lafayette, Square Montholon, St. Vincent de Paul, Northern Railway Terminus, Park of the Buttes Chaumont, Cemetery of Père la Chaise, Prison de la Roquette and Place of Execution, Place de la Bastille and Column of July, Place du Château d'Eau, Porte St. Martin, Porte St. Denis, La Trinité.

SECOND DAY.

St. Augustin, Park Monceau, Arc de Triomphe, Bois de Boulogne, the Lakes, Grand Cascade and Race-course, view of the Citadel of Mont Valérien, Town and Park of St. Cloud, Montretout-Buzenval, Forest of Ville d'Avray, Avenue de Picardie, Versailles, the Grand Trianon and State Carriages.

PALACE, MUSEUM AND PARK OF VERSAILLES, Avenue de Paris, Viroflay, Chaville, Sèvres and its Porcelain Manufactory (exterior), Billancourt, Fortifications of Paris, Viaduct of Auteuil, Palace of the Trocadéro, Seine Embankment, Cours la Reine.

THIRD DAY.

Column Vendôme, Garden of the Tuileries, Institute of France, Mint, Pont Neuf and Statue of Henry IV., Palace of Justice, Ste. Chapelle, Tribunal of Commerce, Conciergerie, Cour de Cassation, St. Germain l'Auxerrois, Palace and Museum of the Louvre, Palais Royal.

Place du Carrousel and Triumphal Arch, Ecole des Beaux Arts, St. Germain des Prés, St. Sulpice, Palace of the Luxembourg, St. Jacques du Haut Pas, Val de Grâce, Carpet Manufactory of the Gobelins, Observatory, Statue of Marshal Ney, Fountain and Gardens of the Luxembourg, Panthéon, Bibliothèque Ste. Geneviève, St. Etienne du Mont, Fontaine Cuvier, Jardin des Plantes, Orleans Railway Terminus, Halle aux Vins, Morgue, Cathedral of Notre Dame, Hôtel Dieu, Place du Châtelet, the new Avenue de l'Opéra.

Monday, Aug. 9th.—Leave Paris, *via* Rouen, Dieppe and Newhaven, for London. (*Midland Grand Hotel.*)
Any passenger preferring the short sea mail route, via Calais and Dover, can be supplied with tickets for that route on payment of the difference of fare.

Tuesday, Aug. 10th.—IN LONDON.

Wednesday, Aug. 11th.—Leave London by evening express train for Glasgow. (*Cockburn Hotel.*)

Thursday Aug. 12th.—Sail from Glasgow or Greenock for New York.

Sunday, Aug. 22d.—Expect to arrive at New York.

The Fare for the First Section includes

First-class Ocean passage, both ways   22 Days.

First-class Hotel accommodation in Great Britain for   11 Days.

First-class Hotel accommodation on the Continent for   18 Days.

Total,   51 Days.

IT ALSO INCLUDES

First-class railway and steamboat traveling for the entire journey; Omnibuses and porterage between Stations and Hotels; free transportation of 60 lbs. of baggage; gratuities to servants; Carriages to Abbotsford; three days Carriage Drives in Paris; fees for sight-seeing, as per Conductor's Programme, services of special local guides where necessary, and also the services of the Conductor, who acts as Interpreter and Manager.

NOTE.—*The Conductor will only pay for carriages ordered by himself, and the services of the guides will be for the whole of the party.*

Hotel provision for each country to be according to the custom of the country, viz.: in Great Britain, Meat Breakfast, Table d'Hote Dinner, Tea, Bedroom, lights, services and attendance. On the Continent: Meat Breakfast, Dinner at Table d'Hote (with or without wine as the hotel provides), Bedrooms, lights and service.

THE SECOND SECTION PROVIDES

FOR VISITING

SCOTLAND, ENGLAND, BELGIUM, THE RHINE DISTRICT, GERMANY, SWITZER- LAND AND FRANCE,

AND INCLUDES

GLASGOW, LOCH LOMOND, LOCH KATRINE, THE TROSSACHS,

STIRLING CASTLE, EDINBURGH, MELROSE, ABBOTSFORD,

LONDON, ANTWERP, BRUSSELS, COLOGNE, THE RHINE, MAYENCE,

WORMS, HEIDELBERG, STUTTGART, MUNICH, LINDAU,

Lake Constance, Zurich, Lucerne,

THE ASCENT OF THE RIGHI, THE BERNESE OBERLAND, GEISSBACH,

Interlaken, Grindelwald, Berne, Lausanne, Lake Leman,

Bouveret, Martigny, The Tete Noir, Chamounix,

MT. BLANC, GENEVA, PARIS, ROUEN, DIEPPE AND BRIGHTON.

65 Days from New York, back to New York, including all necessary expenses,

Fare, $400.

Itinerary of the Second Section.

Saturday, July 3d.—Leave New York, by Anchor Line steamer "Devonia," for Glasgow.

N. B.—We are notified by the Steamship Company that the above-named Steamer is appointed to sail on this date; but we cannot, of course, hold ourselves responsible should any change be made and another Steamer substituted. This, however, is is not likely to occur.

Tuesday, July 13th.—Expect to reach Glasgow. (*Cockburn Hotel.*)

Wednesday, July 14th.—Go by early morning train to Balloch, and take steamer on Loch Lomond for Inversnaid, passing Inch Cailliach, Inch Murrin, and Inch Lonaig. Then be conveyed in coaches to Stronachlacher, and by steamer over Loch Katrine to the Trossachs, past Rob Roy's cave and Ellen's Isle. Coach will be then taken past Loch Achray and Coilantogle Ford to Callander, thence by rail to Stirling, visiting the Royal Castle, etc., and continuing the journey past the Field of Bannockburn and Linlithgow Castle to Edinburgh. (*Cockburn Hotel.*)

Thursday, July 15th.—IN EDINBURGH, visiting Holyrood Palace and Chapel, Edinburgh Castle, the Scott Monument, Calton Hill and the other attractions of Edinburgh.

Friday, July 16th.—Leave by early train, *via* the North British Railway, to Melrose. Carriages will be taken for a visit to the ruined Abbey, and for a five-mile drive to ABBOTSFORD, the home of Sir Walter Scott; then back to Melrose Station, when train will be taken for Carlisle; then by Midland Railway through Leeds, Sheffield, Leicester, Bedford to London. (*Midland Grand Hotel.*)

Saturday, July 17th.
Sunday, July 18th.
Monday, July 19th.
Tuesday, July 20th.

IN LONDON. Owing to the great number of places of interest in the Metropolis, and the diversity of opinions as to which places should be visited, no formal programme for sightseeing will be prepared, but every assistance and information will be afforded to the members of the party by our staff.

Wednesday, July 21st.—Leave London by Flushing or Harwich route at 8.35 p. m. for Antwerp.

Thursday, July 22d.—Arrive at ANTWERP about 10 a. m. (*Hotel d'Europe.*) Visits will be made to the Cathedral, the church of St. Jacques, the church of St. Paul, the Hotel de Ville, Museum, Zoological Gardens, etc., leaving by afternoon train for Brussels. (*Hotel de la Poste.*)

Friday, July 23d.—IN BRUSSELS, during which time the following places will be visited: The Hotel de la Ville, Wiertz Museum, the Palace of the Duke of Arenberg, the Cathedral of St. Gudule, the House of Parliament, etc.

Saturday, July 24th.—Excursion by rail or carriage, to the famous battlefield of Waterloo.

Sunday, July 25th.—A day of rest AT BRUSSELS.

Monday, July 26th.—Leave Brussels by morning express train, *via* Aix la Chapelle, for COLOGNE, arriving early enough to visit the Cathedral and other points of interest. The Cathedral is one of the finest Gothic churches in the world, begun in 1248, was left unfinished from the beginning of the 16th century until 1816; church of St. Ursula (12th century), with the bones of 11,000 martyred virgins; Rathhaus (13th to 16th centuries). (*Hotel Hollande.*)

Tuesday, July 27th.—Leave Cologne by one of the magnificent saloon steamers for MAYENCE. The voyage up the Rhine is one of unsurpassed interest. The banks of this noble river teem with relics of by-gone feudal splendor—ruined castles, whose associations and whose legends awaken every generous feeling, as they glide by on either hand. The beauty and interest of the Rhine scenery are concentrated between Bonn and Bingen, for in quick succession we pass the Seven Mountains, the Drachenfels, Godesberg, Remagen, Rheinech, Andernach, Coblentz, with the Ehrenbreitstein, Boppart, Reinfelz, the Lurlei, Schonberg, Rheinstein, the Maus Thurm, Bingen and Eltville. (*Hotel Hollande.*)

Wednesday, July 28th.—Go from Mayence, *via* Worms, to Heidelberg, stopping for a few hours at Worms to see the famous monument to Luther and other Reformers. (*Hotel d'Europe.*)

Thursday, July 29th.—IN HEIDELBERG, one of the charming spots in

Rhenish Germany ; visit the Schloss and great Tun, the University, Cathedral, etc.

Friday, July 30th.—Go from Heidelberg, *via* Bruchsal, Stuttgart and Ulm (stopping a few hours at Stuttgart, if desirable), to Munich. (*Hotel Bellevue.*)

Saturday, July 31st. Sunday, August 1st. } IN MUNICH, visiting the old Cathedral (built in 1488), the Royal Palace, Royal Bronze Foundry, Art Gallery, etc.

Monday, August 2d.—Leave Munich by morning train for Lindau, crossing Lake Constance by steamer, arriving at ZURICH the same evening. (*Hotel Bellevue.*)

Tuesday, August 3d.—Leave Zurich by afternoon train, *via* Zug, for Lucerne. (*Swan Hotel.*)

Wednesday, August 4th. Thursday, August 5th. } IN LUCERNE, during which time the ascent of the Righi will be made.

At Lucerne may be visited the Lion cut in solid rock, after design by Thorwaldsen, in memory of the Swiss Guards who fell in defending Louis XVI. against the revolutionary mob in Paris, Aug. 10th, 1792. The Glacier Garden, in which are many relics of lacustrine habitations, etc., adjoins the "Lion." The Cathedral, containing one of the best organs in Switzerland, and the quaint church-yard, are full of interest. Old Bridges and Fortifications. The Lake of Lucerne (*Vierwaldstattersee*) is full of wild and picturesque scenery, and is associated with the legend of William Tell.

N. B. Whilst in Lucerne, a special Organ Concert will be given in the Cathedral in honor of the party.

Friday, August 6th.—In carriages on the picturesque Brunig Pass, passing through Sarnen and Lungern, and spending the night at GIESSBACH, and witnessing the illumination of the celebrated Falls. (*Giessbach Hotel.*)

Saturday, August 7th.—By morning boat on the Lake of Brienz to Interlaken, one of the most beautiful spots in Switzerland, and in full view of the Jungfrau. (*Hotel Victoria.*)

Sunday, August 8th.—AT INTERLAKEN. Short and pleasant walks may be made to Heimwehfluh, Unspunnen, Beatenberg, Thurnberg, etc., most of which places afford good views of the Lakes of Thun and Brienz. Carriages will be provided for members of the party desiring to visit Grindelwald.

Monday, August 9th.—By boat over Lake Thun and railway to BERNE. A magnificent panorama of the snowy peaks of the Bernese Alps may be seen from the garden of the Hotel, or from the terrace of the Cathedral, on a fine day. The Cathedral (1421-1573) contains a celebrated organ, on which evening recitals are given. The Clock Tower, Bear Pit, Kindli-fresser, Gothic Church, Rathhaus, &c., constitute the sightseeing of the Capital of Switzerland. (*Hotel Bellevue.*)

Tuesday, August 10th.—By afternoon train to LAUSANNE, situated on the northern bank of the Lake of Geneva. The Cathedral is the grandest Gothic structure in Switzerland. Vevey, Clarens, Castle of Chillon, Villeneuve, Montreux, &c., on the eastern shore of the Lake, may be easily visited from Ouchy, which is the port of Lausanne. A railway worked by hydraulic power connects Lausanne with Ouchy. (*Hotel Gibbon.*)

Wednesday, August 11th.—By steamer across Lake Leman, passing the Castle of Chillon to Bouveret, where train will be taken for Martigny. (*Hotel Clerc.*)

Thursday, August 12th.—Go by mules or carriages over the TETE NOIR to Chamounix. (*Hotel d'Angleterre.*)

Friday, August 13th.—IN THE VALLEY OF CHAMOUNIX. The hotel here commands a magnificent view of MONT BLANC. Excursions may be made to the Montanvert, Mauvais Pas, Mer de Glace, Chapeau, Jardin, Flegere, or to the beautiful gorges of LA DIOZA.

Saturday, August 14th.—Leave by diligence through Sallanches for Geneva. (*Hotels Metropole, du Lac* and *Russie.*)

Sunday, August 15th.—IN GENEVA, visits may be made to the Cathedral where Calvin preached, the Russian Church, Rath, Museum, Rousseau's Island, the meeting of the waters, &c.

Monday, August 16th.—By afternoon express train to Paris. (*Hotels London and New York* and *St. Petersburg.*)

Tuesday, Aug. 17th.
Wednesday, Aug. 18th.   IN PARIS. Three days of which will be devoted
Thursday, Aug. 19th.   to carriage drives, visiting the principal places
Friday, Aug. 20th.   of interest in and around the city, including
Saturday, Aug. 21st.   excursions to St. Cloud, Sevres and Versailles,
Sunday, Aug. 22d.   as per programme in First Section, on page 25.

Monday, Aug. 23d.—Go by day service *via* Rouen, Dieppe and Brighton to London. (*Midland Grand Hotel.*)

Any passenger preferring the short sea mail route, via Calais and Dover, can be supplied with tickets for that route on payment of the difference of fare.

Tuesday, August 24th.—IN LONDON.

Wednesday, August 25th.—Leave by evening express train for Glasgow. (*Cockburn Hotel.*)

Thursday, August 26th.—Leave Glasgow or Greenock by Anchor Line steamer for New York.

Sunday, September 5th.—Expect to arrive at New York.

The Fare for the Second Section includes

First-class Ocean passage both ways,	22 Days.
First-class Hotel accommodation in Great Britain,	10 Days.
First-class Hotel accommodation on the Continent,	33 Days.
	Total, 65 Days.

IT ALSO INCLUDES

First-class railway and steamboat travelling for the entire journey; Omnibuses and Porterage between Stations and Hotels; free transportation of 60 lbs. of baggage; gratuities to servants; Carriages to Abbotsford; Carriage Excursions to Waterloo and Grindelwald; three days Carriage Drives in Paris; fees for sight-seeing as per Conductor's programme; services of special local guides where necessary, and also the services of the Conductor, who acts as interpreter and manager.

NOTE.—*The Conductor will only pay for carriages ordered by himself, and the services of the guides will be for the whole of the party.*

Hotel provision for each country to be according to the custom of the country, viz.: in Great Britain, meat breakfast, table d'hote dinner, tea, bedroom, lights, services and attendance. On the Continent: meat breakfast, dinner at table d'hote (with or without wine as the hotel provides), bedrooms, light and service.

THE THIRD SECTION PROVIDES

FOR VISITING

SCOTLAND, ENGLAND, BELGIUM, THE RHINE DISTRICT,

Germany, Switzerland, France and Italy,

AND INCLUDES

Glasgow, Loch Lomond, Loch Katrine, the Trossachs, Stirling Castle, Edinburgh, Melrose, Abbotsford, London, Antwerp, Brussels, Cologne, the Rhine, Mayence, Worms, Heidelberg, Stuttgart, Munich, Lindau, Lake Constance, Zurich, Lucerne, the Ascent of the Righi,

The Bernese Oberland, Giessbach, Interlaken, the Grindelwald, Berne, Lausanne,

LAKE LEMAN, BOUVERET, MARTIGNY, THE TETE NOIR, CHAMOUNIX, MONT BLANC,

Geneva, the Mont Cenis Tunnel, Turin, Genoa, Pisa, Rome, Naples, Pompeii, Florence, Venice, Milan, Lake Como, Lugano, the St. Gothard Pass, Fluelen, Bale, Paris, Rouen, Dieppe and Brighton.

86 Days from New York, back to New York, including all necessary expenses.

Fare, $500.

Itinerary of the Third Section.

Saturday, July 3d.—Leave New York by Anchor Line steamer "Devonia," for Glasgow.

N. B.—We are notified by the Steamship Company that the above-named Steamer is appointed to sail on this date; but we cannot, of course, hold ourselves responsible should any change be made, and another Steamer substituted. This, however, is not likely to occur.

Tuesday, July 13th.— Expect to reach Glasgow. (*Cockburn Hotel.*)

Wednesday, July 14th.- Go by early morning train to Balloch, and take steamer on Loch Lomond for Inversnaid, passing Inch Cailliach, Inch Murrin, and Inch Lonaig. Then be conveyed in coaches to Stronachlacher, and by steamer over Loch Katrine to the Trossachs, past Rob Roy's Cave and Ellen's Isle. Coach will be then taken past Loch Achray and Coilantogle Ford to Callander, thence by rail to Stirling, visiting the Royal Castle, etc., and continuing the journey past the Field of Bannockburn and Linlithgow Castle to Edinburgh. (*Cockburn Hotel.*)

Thursday, July 15th.—IN EDINBURGH, visiting Holyrood Palace and Chapel, Edinburgh Castle, the Scott Monument, Calton Hill, and the other attractions of Edinburgh.

Friday, July 16th.—Leave by special early train, *via* the North British Railway, to Melrose. Carriages will be taken for a visit to the ruined Abbey, and for a five-mile drive to **ABBOTSFORD**, the home of Sir Walter Scott; then back to Melrose Station, when special train will be taken for Carlisle; then by Midland Railway through Leeds, Sheffield, Leicester, Bedford to London. (*Midland Grand Hotel.*)

Saturday, July 17th.
Sunday, July 18th.
Monday, July 19th.
Tuesday, July 20th.

IN LONDON. Owing to the great number of places of interest in the metropolis, and the diversity of opinions as to which places should be visited, no formal programme for sight-seeing will be prepared, but every assistance and information will be afforded to the members of the party by our staff.

Wednesday, July 21st.—Leave London by Flushing or Harwich route at 8.35 p. m. for Antwerp.

Thursday, July 22d.—Arrive at **ANTWERP** about 10 a. m. (*Hotel d'Europe.*) Visits will be made to the Cathedral, the church of St. Jacques, the church of St. Paul, the Hotel de Ville, Museum, Zoological Gardens, etc., leaving by afternoon train for Brussels. (*Hotel de la Poste.*)

Friday, July 23d.—IN **BRUSSELS**, during which time the following places will be visited: The Hotel de la Ville, Wiertz Museum, the Palace of the Duke of Arenberg, the Cathedral of St. Gudule, the House of Parliament, etc.

Saturday, July 24th.—Excursion by rail or carriage to the famous battlefield of Waterloo.

Sunday, July 25th.—A day of rest at **BRUSSELS**.

Monday, July 26th.—Leave Brussels by morning express train, *via* Aix la Chapelle, for **COLOGNE**, arriving early enough to visit the Cathedral and other points of interest. The Cathedral is one of the finest Gothic churches in the world, begun in 1248, was left unfinished from the beginning of the 16th century until 1816; church of St. Ursula (12th century), with the bones of 11,000 martyred virgins; Rathhaus (13th to 16th centuries.) (*Hotel Hollande.*)

Tuesday, July 27th.—Leave Cologne by one of the magnificent saloon steamers for **MAYENCE**. The voyage up the Rhine is one of unsurpassed interest. The banks of this noble river teem with relics of by-gone feudal splendor—ruined castles, whose associations and whose legends awaken every generous feeling, as they glide by on either hand. The beauty and interest of the Rhine scenery are concentrated between Bonn and Bingen, for in quick succession we pass the Seven Mountains, the Drachenfels, Godesberg, Remagen, Rheineck, Andernach, Coblentz, with the Ehrenbreitstein, Boppart, Reinfelz, the Lurlei, Schonberg, Rheinstein, the Maus Thurm, Bingen and Eltville. (*Hotel Hollande.*)

Wednesday, July 28th.—Go from Mayence, *via* Worms, to Heidelberg, stopping for a few hours at Worms to see the celebrated monument to Luther and other Reformers. (*Hotel d'Europe.*)

Thursday, July 29th.—IN **HEIDELBERG**, one of the charming spots in Rhenish Germany, visit the Schloss and great Tun, the University, Cathedral, etc.

Friday, July 30th.—Go from Heidelberg, *via* Bruchsal, Stuttgart and Ulm, (stopping a few hours at Stuttgart, if desirable), to Munich. (*Hotel Bellevue.*)

Saturday, July 31st. ⎱ IN MUNICH, visiting the old Cathedral (built in
Sunday, August 1st. ⎰ 1488), the Royal Palace, Royal Bronze Foundry, Art Gallery, etc.

Monday, August 2d.—Leave Munich by morning train for Lindau, crossing Lake Constance by steamer, arriving at ZURICH the same evening. (*Hotel Bellevue.*)

Tuesday, August 3d.—Leave ZURICH by afternoon train, *via* Zug, for Lucerne. (*Swan Hotel.*)

Wednesday, August 4th. ⎱ IN LUCERNE, during which time the ascent of
Thursday, August 5th. ⎰ the Righi will be made.

At Lucerne may be visited the Lion cut in solid rock, after design by Thorwaldsen, in memory of the Swiss Guards who fell in defending Louis XVI. against the revolutionary mob in Paris, Aug. 10th, 1792. The Glacier Garden, in which are many relics of lacustrine habitations, &c., adjoins the "Lion." The Cathedral, containing one of the best organs in Switzerland, and the quaint Church-yard, are full of interest. Old Bridges and Fortifications. The Lake of Lucerne (*Vierwaldstattersee*) is full of wild and picturesque scenery, and is associated with the legend of William Tell.

N. B.—Whilst in Lucerne a special Organ Concert will be given in the Cathedral in honor of the party.

Friday, August 6th.—In carriages on the picturesque Brunig Pass, passing through Sarnen and Lungern, and spending the night at Giessbach, and witnessing the illumination of the celebrated Falls. (*Giessbach Hotel.*)

Saturday, August 7th.—By morning boat on the Lake of Brienz to Interlaken, one of the most beautiful spots in Switzerland, and in full view of the Jungfrau. (*Hotel Victoria.*)

Sunday, August 8th.—AT INTERLAKEN. Short and pleasant walks may be made to Heimwehfluh, Unspunnen, Beatenberg, Thurnberg, &c., most of which places afford good views of the Lakes of Thun and Brienz. Carriages will be provided for members of the party desiring to visit Grindelwald.

Monday, August 9th.—By boat over Lake Thun, and railway to BERNE. A magnificent panorama of the snowy peaks of the Bernese Alps may be seen from the garden of the Hotel, or from the terrace of the Cathedral, on a fine day. The Cathedral (1421-1573) contains a celebrated organ, on which evening recitals are given. The Clock Tower, Bear Pit, Kindli-fresser, Gothic Church, Rathhaus, etc., constitute the sight-seeing of the Capital of Switzerland. (*Hotel Bellevue.*)

Tuesday, August 10th.—By afternoon train to LAUSANNE, situated on the northern bank of the Lake of Geneva. The Cathedral is the grandest Gothic structure in Switzerland. Vevey, Clarens, Castle of Chillon, Villeneuve, Montreux, &c., on the eastern shore of the Lake, may be easily visited from Ouchy, which is the port of Lausanne. A railway worked by hydraulic power connects Lausanne with Ouchy. (*Hotel Gibbon.*)

Wednesday, August 11th.—By steamer across Lake Leman, passing the Castle of Chillon to Bouveret, where train will be taken for Martigny. (*Hotel Clerc.*)

Thursday, August 12th.—Go by mules or carriages over the TETE NOIR to Chamounix. (*Hotel de l'Angleterre.*)

Friday, August 13th.—IN THE VALLEY OF CHAMOUNIX. The hotel here commands a magnificent view of MONT BLANC. Excursions may be made to the Montanvert, Mauvais Pas, Mer de Glace, Chapeau, Jardin, Flegere, or to the beautiful gorges of LA DIOZA.

Saturday, August 14th.—Leave by diligence through Sallanche for Geneva. (*Hotels Metropole, du Lac and Russie.*)

Sunday, August 15th.—IN GENEVA. Visits may be made to the Cathedral where Calvin preached, the Russian Church, Rath, Museum, Rousseau's Island, the Meeting of the Waters, etc.

Monday, Aug. 16th.—Leave Geneva by morning train for Turin, arriving at 6.20 p. m. (*Hotels Trombetta and d'Angleterre.*)

Tuesday, Aug. 17.—Go by noon train to Genoa. (*Hotel de la Ville.*)

Wednesday, Aug. 18th.—IN GENOA, visiting the Cathedral, Church of the Annunziata, Palace of the Doges, Public Gardens, etc.

Thursday, Aug. 19th.—Leave Genoa by the Riviera Railway *via* Spezia, for PISA. (*Hotel de Londres.*)

Friday Aug. 20th.—The morning will be spent in viewing the Cathedral, Baptistry, Leaning Tower, Campo Santo, etc., leaving by noon train for Rome. (*Hotels d'Allemagne and Continental.*)

Saturday, Aug. 21st. ⎫ IN ROME, three days of which will be devoted to
Sunday, Aug. 22d.   ⎪ carriage excursions, under the superintendence of
Monday, Aug. 23d.   ⎬ Mr. Shakspere Wood, the eminent archæologist, ac-
Tuesday, Aug. 24th. ⎭ cording to the following programme :

FIRST DAY.

THE PALATINE.—The Seven Hills; remains of the Walls of Romulus and Port Mugonia; remains of Temples and Edifices of the early Republic; remains of Houses of the Republican period; House of Tiberius Claudius Nero, with Fresco paintings.

THE PALACE OF THE CÆSARS.—Site of the House of Augustus; Palace of Tiberius; substructions of the Palace of Caligula, and Porticos built by him to the Domus Tiberiana; great suite of State rooms, built by Domitian; Lararium, Basilica, Triclinium, &c.; Intermontium; great Stadium of Domitian; gigantic Porticos of Septimius Severus; site of Septizonium, &c., &c.

BASILICA OF CONSTANTINE.

ARCH OF TITUS.—Bas-relief of Soldiers carrying Seven-branched Candlestick, &c.

(AFTER LUNCH.)

THE COLOSSEUM.

TEMPLE OF VENUS AND ROME.

REMAINS OF DOMUS TRANSITORIA OF NERO.

ARCH OF CONSTANTINE.

META SUDANS.

TEMPLE OF VESTA.

THE PANTHEON.

TEMPLE OF FORTUNA VIRILIS.

PONTE ROTTO and View along the Tiber.

THE CLOACA MAXIMA.

THEATRE OF MARCELLUS.

THE PORTICO OF OCTAVIA.

SECOND DAY.

THE FORUM ROMANUM.—Via Sacra; Vicus Tuscus; Clivus Capitolinus; Temples of Castor and Pollux, the Deified Julius, Saturn, Vespasian, Concord; the Basilica Julia; Honorary Monuments, the Pedestal of Domitian's Statue, Column of Phocas; Rostrum; Arch of Septimius Severus; Portico of the Deii Consentes; the Tabularium.

THE TARPEIAN ROCK.

THE MAMERTINE PRISON.

THE FORA OF THE EMPERORS Augustus, Nerva, Trajan.

(AFTER LUNCH.)

THE GOLDEN HOUSE OF NERO.
BATHS OF TITUS.
BASILICA OF ST. CLEMENT; the Basilica of the Twelfth Century; the now subterranean Basilica of the Fourth Century; marvelously preserved Frescoes; House of Clement; Temple of Mithras; remains of a grand edifice of the Republican period, superimposed on a portion of the wall of the Kings, beneath the subterranean Basilica.
BASILICA OF ST. JOHN LATERAN.
THE SCALA SANCTA.
AQUEDUCT OF NERO.
BASILICA OF ST. PAUL, Outside the Walls.

THIRD DAY.

VATICAN MUSEUM OF SCULPTURE.
THE SIXTINE CHAPEL.—Michael Angelo's "Last Judgment."
STANZE AND LOGGIE OF RAPHAEL.
VATICAN PICTURE GALLERY.—"The Transfiguration ;" "Communion of St. Jerome ;" "Madonna di Foligno," &c., &c.

(AFTER LUNCH.)

BATHS OF CARACALLA;   PORTA ST. SEBASTIANO;
COLOMBARIA.

THE APPIAN WAY.—Tombs of Geta, Priscilla, Cecilia Metella, Seneca, the Cotta Family, &c., &c.; Tumuli of the Horatii and Curiatii; the Villa of the Quintilii; the Ustrinum; the Circus of Romulus; the Catacombs.

Wednesday, August 25th.—Leave Rome by morning train for Naples. (*Hotels de Russie* and *Metropole*.)

Thursday, August 26th.
Friday, August 27th.
} IN NAPLES, during which time the party will visit the principal places of interest in the city and surroundings, including an excursion to Pompeii.

Saturday, August 28th.—Leave Naples for Florence, *via* Rome. (*Hotels: New York, d'Europe, and Russie*.)

Sunday, Aug. 29th.
Monday, Aug. 30th.
} IN FLORENCE, during which time visits will be made to the tombs of the Medicis, the Cathedral and Baptistry, Church of Santa Croce (the Westminster Abbey of Italy), the Uffizi Gallery, Palaces of the Signoria and Pitti, etc., etc.

Tuesday, August 31st.—Leave Florence by morning train for Venice, *via* Bologna. The railway line between Florence and Bologna, which intersects the Tuscan Apennines, is one of the grandest in Europe. Bridges, tunnels (45 in all), and galleries are traversed in uninterrupted succession. Beautiful views are obtained of the valleys and gorges of the Appenines and of the luxuriant plains of Tuscany, "the Garden of Italy." (*Hotel Victoria*.)

Wednesday, Sept. 1st.
Thursday, Sept. 2d.
} IN VENICE, during which time gondolas will be provided for visiting the most important points of interest, including the Church of St. Marc, Royal Palace, the Palace of the Doges, the Bridge of Sighs, State Prisons, the principal Churches, Museums, Art Galleries, the Islands of the Lagoons, the Lido, etc., etc.

Friday Sept. 3.—Leave Venice for Milan, *via* Verona, Desenzano, Brescia, &c. Between Peschiera and Desenzano a view of the picturesque Lake of Garda is obtained. (*Hotel de Milan.*)

Saturday, Sept. 4.—IN MILAN. Spend the morning visiting the Cathedral dedicated to Marie Nascenti, one of the finest specimens of Gothic architecture in the world. The Gallery Vittorio Emanuele or Public Arcade, which is one of the most spacious and attractive of its kind in existence. The Arch of Peace, the Brera Collection of Pictures and Statues, the Church of Santa Maria delle Grazie—containing, in the Monastery, the celebrated "Last Supper" of Leonardo da Vinci—leaving by afternoon train for Como and Cernobio. (*Hotel de la Reine d'Angleterre.*)

Sunday, Sept. 5th.—To be spent on the banks of the LAKE OF COMO, the most charming of the Italian Lakes, and one of the loveliest spots in Europe.

Monday, Sept. 6th.—By morning steamer to Menaggio, Porlezza, and Lugano, leaving by diligence at 4.26 p. m. for Bellinzona, rail to Biasca, and from thence by diligence over the famous St. Gothard Pass (6935 feet above the sea), to Fluelen, reaching there the following afternoon.

Tuesday, Sept. 7th.—From Fluelen by steamer on the Lake of the Four Cantons to Lucerne. (*Swan Hotel.*)

Wednesday, Sept. 8th.—Travel to Paris *via* Bale. (*Hotels London and New York and St. Petersburg.*)

Thursday, Sept. 9th.
Friday, Sept. 10th.
Saturday, Sept.11th.
Sunday, Sept. 12th.
{ **IN PARIS,** three days of which will be devoted to carriage drives, visiting the principal places of interest in and around the city, including an excursion to St. Cloud, Sevres and Versailles, as per programme in first section on page 25.

Monday, Sept.13th.—Leave by day or night service, *via* Rouen, Dieppe and Brighton, for London. (*Midland Grand Hotel.*)

Any passenger preferring the short sea mail route, via Calais and Dover, can be supplied with tickets for that route on payment of the difference of fare.

Tuesday, Sept. 14th.—IN LONDON.

Wednesday, Sept. 15th.--Leave by evening express train for Glasgow. (*Cockburn Hotel.*)

Thursday, Sept. 16th.---Leave Glasgow or Greenock by Anchor Line steamer for New York.

Sunday, Sept. 26th.---Expect to arrive at New York.

The Fare for the Third Section includes

First-class Ocean passage both ways,   22 Days.
First-class Hotel accommodation in Great Britain, 10 Days.
First-class Hotel accommodation on the Continent, 54 Days.

Total, 86 Days.

IT ALSO INCLUDES.

First-class railway and steamboat traveling for the entire journey; Omnibuses and porterage between Stations and Hotels; free transportation of 60 lbs. of Baggage; gratuities to servants; Carriages to Abbotsford; Carriage Excursions to Waterloo and Grindelwald; three days carriages in Rome and the services of Mr. Shakspere Wood ; trip to Pompeii ; gondolas for one day in Venice ; three days Carriage Drives in Paris; fees for sight-seeing, as per Conductor's programme; services of special local guides where necessary, and also the services of the Conductor, who acts as Interpreter and Manager.

NOTE.—*The Conductor will only pay for carriages ordered by himself, and the services of the Guides will be for the whole of the party.*

Hotel provision for each country to be according to the custom of the country, viz.: In Great Britain, Meat Breakfast, Table d'Hote Dinner, Tea, Bedroom, lights, service, and attendance. On the Continent: Meat Breakfast, Dinner at Table d'Hote (with or without wine as the Hotel provides), Bedrooms, lights and service.

A Deposit of Fifty Dollars

is required from each person who decides to go with either of the sections of this tour ; when the deposit is made, the name is registered, and the berths are allotted in the exact order of these deposits, the earliest depositors, of course, receiving the best berths.

Forty dollars of this deposit may be withdrawn up to June 15th, after which time the whole amount is due.

How to Join the Party.

Persons desirous of joining this party should write as early as possible, enclosing draft on any bank or postal order made payable to the order of Thos. Cook & Son, *and stating distinctly which section they wish to join.* We will, upon receipt of the same, return a "Deposit Receipt" and a plan of the steamer, showing the location of the berths we can offer. Should the choice of berths be left to us, we will use our best judgment in the interest of each, and advise them at once. The balance of the money can be paid any time after June 15th.

Extension of Time.

The steamship tickets for these tours are good to return any time during the year on any steamer of the Anchor Line which sails from Glasgow.

Breaks in the Journey can be made at almost any principal point, and as the return steamship tickets are good for one year, any of the members of this party can remain in Europe at their discretion. The whole amount of fare must be paid before starting, but they can receive back the value of their unused tickets and Hotel Coupons, less 10 per cent., (*Swiss Traveling Tickets excepted*) at the Chief London Office, or they can be exchanged for tickets to other points at their full value.

On the return from the Continent, if any wish to extend their tour to the English Lakes, Scotland, and Ireland, taking the steamer at Moville, quotations will be given by Messrs. Thos. Cook & Son ; and if a party of 10 or more is made up for such supplementary tour, a Conductor will be sent with them, without extra charge.

Other Lines of Steamers.

To any who wish to avail themselves of this Tour, and join this party, but prefer some other line of steamers, we can accommodate them, and will give them a special quotation either higher or lower, according to the line preferred. We will also, for those who have engaged steamship passage, give quotations, and book them from Liverpool, London or Paris.

Detours.

Any member of the above party will be allowed to leave the main party, to visit other localities, provided early notice be given to the Conductor, so that engagements for hotel accommodations may not be violated. Hotel coupons will be supplied those who so leave the party, for the number of days they expect to be absent. Any unused coupons to be redeemed at the advertised rate.

LETTERS may be addressed to any member of the party, care of Thomas Cook & Son, Ludgate Circus, London, and such letters will be carefully forwarded to the Conductor of the party for delivery.

MONEY, LETTERS OF CREDIT AND CIRCULAR CHECKS are issued by us, at current rates, in the denomination of five or ten pounds sterling each, and are payable at nearly every point on the route, or will be cashed by the Conductor as required, and in the currency of the country where the party happens to be at the time.

Cautionary Proviso, applying to all Sections.

The liability of Alpine roads and railroads in the neighborhood of mountains to damage from storms and other influences beyond human control, renders it necessary that we should announce that we cannot be responsible for detention or expenses incurred by deviation of routes occasioned by circumstances of this nature, nor for delays or deviation that may be caused through the railways being required for military purposes.

The most that Companies will do under such circumstances is to repay the value of any tickets or proportion of tickets not used for lines thus rendered impassable; and all claims in such cases must be sent in writing, accompanied by the unused tickets, within one-month from the date for which such tickets were available.

Baggage.— Whilst anxious to render all possible assistance to travellers in the transport, care and registration of baggage, Thos. Cook & Son cannot admit responsibility in cases of detention, stray conveyance, damage to or loss of baggage. In all cases of transference it is necessary that baggage should be identified by its owners, especially on entering and leaving hotels and railway stations; and whenever baggage is subject to customs examination, its owners should be present to answer for it.

N. B.—Great care will be taken in the registration and conveyance of the trunks or portmanteaus of the parties whilst travelling with the Conductor; but it must be distinctly understood that all small packages, such as handbags, umbrellas, travelling rugs, &c., must remain entirely under the control of the passenger.

THOS. COOK & SON,

261 Broadway, New York.

COOK'S MIDSUMMER EXCURSION

TO EUROPE.

PROGRAMME

OF A

Special Personally-Conducted Party,

LEAVING

NEW YORK, SATURDAY, JULY 31st, 1880,

By Steamship " City of Richmond," of the Inman Line,

GIVING CHOICE OF THREE ROUTES,

INCLUDING VISITS TO THE MOST INTERESTING CITIES OF

*ENGLAND, FRANCE, BELGIUM, THE RHINE, GER-
MANY, SWITZERLAND AND ITALY, AND INCLUDING
ALSO THE VALLEY OF CHAMOUNIX, MONT
BLANC, THE SIMPLON PASS, &c., &c.*

Section	I. Providing for	**34 Days' Tour**	-	**$210**	
Section	II. "	" **50 Days'** "	-	310	
Section	III. "	" **64 Days'** "	-	410	

UNDER THE MANAGEMENT OF

→⁑THOMAS COOK & SON.⁑←

Originators of the Tourist and Excursion System (Established 1841), and only successful Con-
ductors of Tours and Excursions to all parts of the Globe.
Specially appointed by His Royal Highness the Prince of Wales Sole Passenger Agents to the
Royal British Commission, Vienna 1873, Philadelphia 1876, and Paris 1878.

CHIEF OFFICE, LUDGATE CIRCUS, LONDON.
CHIEF AMERICAN OFFICE, 261 BROADWAY, NEW YORK, P. O. Box 4197.

INTRODUCTION.

The success which has attended the Midsummer parties in previous years, justifies us in organizing a similar tour annually. We have again the pleasure of announcing that we have made a special arrangement with the Inman Steamship Company for the conveyance of this party from New York to Liverpool, on the steamship "City of Richmond," one of the largest and finest steamers of their fleet.

Under this special arrangement we are enabled to quote for this party the lowest possible fares, giving the choice of three routes.

Special attention is called to the first section, which embraces Liverpool, London, Paris, etc., the whole trip lasting 34 days. We can especially recommend this section to those who, having but little time at their disposal, wish to have the benefit of the sea journey and to make a short stay in London and Paris.

Those having more time at their disposal cannot fail to appreciate the itineraries of the second and third sections.

If after the perusal of the following itineraries further information is required, please address

THOMAS COOK & SON,

261 Broadway, New York.

THE FIRST SECTION PROVIDES

FOR VISITING

LIVERPOOL, LONDON, ROUEN, PARIS, VERSAILLES, DIEPPE, NEWHAVEN AND BRIGHTON.

34 Days from New York, back to New York, including all necessary expenses.

Fare, $210.

Itinerary of the First Section.

Saturday, July 31st.—Leave New York by steamship "City of Richmond" at 1 p. m.

N. B.—We are notified by the Steamship Company that the above-named Steamer is appointed to sail on this date; but we cannot, of course, hold ourselves responsible should any change be made and another Steamer substituted. This, however, is not likely to occur.

Tuesday, Aug. 10th.—Expect to land at Liverpool and proceed by express train on the Midland Railway to London, going through the celebrated Derbyshire Peak District, and passing Derby, Leicester, Bedford, etc., stopping at the Midland Grand Hotel, in London, one of the finest and largest hotels in the world.

Wednesday, Aug. 11th.
Thursday, Aug. 12th.
Friday, Aug. 13th.

IN LONDON.
Owing to the great number of places of interest in the Metropolis, and the diversity of opinions as to which places should be visited, no formal programme for sight-seeing will be prepared, but every assistance and information will be afforded to the members of the party by our staff.

Saturday, Aug. 14th.—Leave London for Paris, *via* Newhaven and Dieppe, by 8 p. m. train from London Bridge Station.

Passengers preferring the short sea mail route via Dover and Calais can be supplied with tickets for that route on payment of the difference of fare.

Sunday, Aug. 15th.—Arrive in Paris. (*Hotels St. Petersburg* and *London and New York.*)

Monday, Aug. 16th.
Tuesday, Aug. 17th.
Wednesday, Aug. 18th.
Thursday, Aug. 19th.
Friday, Aug. 20th.

IN PARIS, three days of which will be devoted to carriage drives, visiting the principal places of interest in and around the city, including an excursion to St. Cloud, Sevres and Versailles, according to the following programme:

FIRST DAY.

New French Opera, Grand Boulevarts, Madeleine, Place de la Concorde and Obelisk of Luxor, Champs Elysées, Palace of Industry, Palace of the Elysée, Arc de Triomphe de l'Etoile, Exhibition Buildings, Ecole Militaire, Invalides and Tomb of Napoleon, Ministry of Foreign Affairs, Palace Bourbon, Pont de la Concorde, Palace of the Legion of Honor, Palace of the Council of State (ruins), Tuileries, Palais Royal.

Bibliothèque Nationale, Bourse, Rue Lafayette, Square Montholon, St. Vincent de Paul, Northern Railway Terminus, Park of the Buttes Chaumont, Cemetery of Père la Chaise, Prison de la Roquette and Place of Execution, Place de la Bastile and Column of July, Place du Chateau d'Eau, Porte St. Martin, Porte St. Denis, La Trinité.

SECOND DAY.

St. Augustin, Park Monceau, Arc de Triomphe, Bois de Boulogne, the Lakes, Grand Cascade and Race-course, view of the Citadel of Mont Valérian, Town and Park of St. Cloud, Montretout-Buzenval, Forest of Ville d'Avray, Avenue de Picardie, Versailles, the Grand Trianon and State Carriages.

PALACE MUSEUM AND PARK OF VERSAILLES, Avenue de Paris, Viroflay, Chaville, Sèvres and its Porcelain Manufactory (exterior), Billancourt, Fortifications of Paris. Viaduct of Auteuil, Palace of the Trocadéro, Seine Embankment, Cours la Reine.

THIRD DAY.

Column Vèndome, Garden of the Tuileries, Institute of France, Mint, Pont Neuf and Statue of Henry IV., Palace of Justice, Ste. Chapelle, Tribunal of Commerce, Conciergerie, Cour de Cassation, St. Germain l'Auxerrois, Palace and Museum of the Louvre, Palais Royal.

Place du Carrousel and Triumphal Arch, Ecole des Beaux Arts, St. Germain des Près, St. Sulpice, Palace of the Luxembourg, St. Jacques du Haut Pas, Val de Grace, Carpet Manufactory of the Gobelins; Observatory, Statue of Marshal Ney, Fountain and Gardens of the Luxembourg, Panthéon, Bibliothèque, Ste. Généviève, St. Etienne du Mont, Fontaine Cuvier, Jardin des Plantes, Orleans Railway Terminus, Halle aux Vins, Morgue, Cathedral of Notre Dame, Hôtel Dieu, Place du Chatelet, the new Avenue de l'Opéra.

Saturday, August 21st.—Leave Paris by morning express train for London, going through the beautiful Valley of the Seine, passing Rouen and Dieppe, taking steamer at this last place for Newhaven, reaching London same evening.

Passengers who may so desire can leave Paris on Friday evening and spend part of Saturday in Brighton, joining the party again on Saturday evening for London. (*Midland Grand Hotel.*)

Sunday, Aug. 22d.—IN LONDON.

Monday, Aug. 23d.—Proceed by morning express train to LIVERPOOL and spend the remainder of the day visiting the docks, Royal Exchange and other places of interest. (*Washington Hotel.*)

Tuesday, August 24th.—Sail from Liverpool on steamship "City of Chester" for Queenstown.

Wednesday, Aug. 25th.—Arrive at Queenstown, take mails and sail for New York.

Saturday, September 4th.—Expect to arrive in New York.

Passengers desiring to remain a week longer in Paris or London, can do so by paying for the additional hotel accommodation required.

The Fare for the First Section includes

First-class Ocean passage both ways,	20 Days.
First-class Hotel accommodation in Great Britain,	7 Days.
First-class Hotel accommodation on the Continent,	7 Days.
	Total, 34 Days.

IT ALSO INCLUDES

First-class railway and steamboat traveling for the entire journey; Omnibuses and Porterage between Stations and Hotels; free transportation of 60 lbs. of

Baggage; gratuities to Servants; three days' carriage drives in Paris; fees for sight-seeing as per Conductor's programme; services of special local guides where necessary; and also the services of the Conductor, who acts as Interpreter and Manager.

NOTE—*The Conductor will only pay for carriages ordered by himself, and the services of the Guides will be for the whole of the party.*

Hotel provision for each country to be according to the custom of the country, viz.: in Great Britain, Meat Breakfast, Table d'Hote Dinner, Tea, Bedroom, lights, services and attendance. On the Continent: Meat Breakfast, Dinner at Table d'Hote (with or without wine as the Hotel provides), Bedrooms, lights and service.

THE SECOND SECTION PROVIDES

FOR VISITING

England, Belgium, the Rhine District, Germany, Switzerland and France,

AND INCLUDES

Liverpool, London, Antwerp, Brussels, Cologne, Bonn, The Rhine, Bingen, Heidelberg, Bale, Lucerne, The Ascent of the Righi, The Brunig Pass, Giessbach, Interlaken, Grindelwald, Thun, Berne, Lausanne, Ouchy, Lake Leman, Geneva, Paris, Versailles, Rouen, Dieppe, Newhaven and Brighton.

50 Days from New York, back to New York, including all necessary expenses.

Fare, $810.

— ◆ —

Itinerary of the Second Section.

Saturday, July 31st—Leave New York by steamship "City of Richmond" at 1 p. m.

N. B.— We are notified by the Steamship Company that the above-named Steamer is appointed to sail on this date; but we cannot, of course, hold ourselves responsible should any change be made and another Steamer substituted. This, however, is not likely to occur.

Tuesday, August 10th.-- Expect to land at Liverpool and proceed to London by Midland Railway, going through the celebrated Derbyshire Peak district, and passing Derby, Leicester, Bedford, etc. (*Midland Grand Hotel.*)

Wednesday, Aug. 11th.
Thursday, Aug. 12th.

{ **IN LONDON.**
Owing to the great number of places of interest in the Metropolis and the diversity of opinions as to which places should be visited, no formal programme for sight-seeing will be prepared, but every assistance and information will be afforded to the members of the party by our staff.

Friday, Aug. 13th.—Leave London at 8.35 p. m., *via* Queenboro' and Flushing, for Antwerp.

Saturday, Aug. 14th.—Arrive at **ANTWERP** about 10 a. m. (*Hotel d' Europe.*) Visits will be made to the Cathedral, the church of St. Jacques, the church of St. Paul, the Hotel de Ville, Museum, Zoological Gardens, etc., leaving by afternoon train for Brussels. (*Hotel de la Poste.*)

Sunday, Aug. 15th.—IN BRUSSELS. The principal sights of this city are the Hotel de la Ville, Wiertz Museum, the palace of the Duke of Arenberg, the Cathedral of St. Gudule, the House of Parliament.

Monday, Aug. 16th.—Leave Brussels by morning express train, *via* Aix la Chapelle, for **COLOGNE,** arriving early enough to visit the Cathedral and other points of interest; the Cathedral is one of the finest Gothic churches in the world, begun in 1248, was left unfinished from the beginning of the 16th century until 1816; church of St. Ursula (12th century), with the bones of 11,000 martyred virgins ; Rathhaus (13th to 16th centuries). (*Hotel Hollande.*)

Tuesday, Aug. 17th.—By morning train to Bonn, where take steamer for Bingen. The voyage on one of the magnificent steamers up or down the Rhine is one of unsurpassed interest. The banks of this noble river teem with relics of bygone feudal splendor; ruined castles, whose associations and whose legends awaken every generous feeling as they glide by on either hand. The beauty and the interest of Rhine scenery are concentrated between Bonn and Bingen; for in quick succession we pass the Seven Mountains, the Drachenfels, Godesberg, Remagen, Rheineck, Andernach, Coblentz, with Ehrenbreitstein, Boppart, Rheinfelz, the Lurlei, Schonberg, Gutenfels, Bacharach, Lorch, Rheinstein, the Maus Thurm. At Bingen the party will land and proceed by train to Heidelberg. (*Hotel d' Europe.*)

Wednesday, Aug. 18th.—IN HEIDELBERG, one of the charming spots in Rhenish Germany, visit the Schloss and great Tun, the University, Cathedral, etc.

Thursday, Aug. 19th.—Proceed by morning express train to **BALE.** (*Hotel Trois Rois.*)

Friday, Aug. 20th.—Travel to Lucerne. (*Swan Hotel.*)

Saturday, Aug. 21st. { **IN LUCERNE,** during which time the ascent of the
Sunday, Aug. 22d. } Righi will be made.

At Lucerne may be visited the Lion cut in solid rock, after design by Thorwaldsen, in memory of the Swiss Guards who fell in defending Louis XVI. against the revolutionary mob in Paris, Aug. 10th, 1792. The Glacier Garden, in which are many relics of lacustrine habitations, &c., adjoins the "Lion." The Cathedral, containing one of the best organs in Switzerland, and the quaint Church-yard, are full of interest. Old Bridges and Fortifications. The Lake of Lucerne (*Vierwaldstättersee*) is full of wild and picturesque scenery, and is associated with the legend of William Tell.

Monday, Aug. 23d.—In carriages on the picturesque Brunig Pass, passing through Sarnen and Lungern, and spending the night at **GIESSBACH,** and witnessing the illumination of the celebrated Falls. (*Giessbach Hotel.*)

Tuesday, Aug. 24th.—By boat on the Lake of Brienz to Interlaken, one of the most beautiful spots in Switzerland, and in full view of the Jungfrau. (*Hotel Victoria.*)

Wednesday, Aug. 25th.—AT INTERLAKEN. Carriages will be provided for an excursion to Grindelwald, to see the wonderful glaciers. Short and pleasant walks may be made to Heinwehflüh, Unspunnen, Beatenberg, Thurnberg, &c., most of which places afford good views of the Lakes of Thun and Brienz.

Thursday, Aug. 26th.—By boat over Lake Thun and railway to **BERNE.** (*Hotel Bellevue.*) A magnificent panorama of the snowy peaks of the Bernese Alps may be seen from the garden of the Hotel, or from the terrace of the Cathedral, on a fine day. The Cathedral (1421-1573) contains a celebrated organ, on which evening recitals are given. The Clock Tower, Bear Pit, Kindli-fresser, Gothic Church, Rathaus, &c., constitute the sight-seeing of the capital of Switzerland.

Friday, Aug. 27th.—By morning express train to **LAUSANNE,** thence by rail to Ouchy, where take steamer on the Lake Leman for Geneva. (*Hotels du Lac and Russie.*)

Saturday, Aug. 28th. } **IN GENEVA ;** visits may be made to the Cathedral
Sunday, Aug. 29th. } where Calvin preached, the Russian Church, Rath, Museum, Rousseau's Island, the meeting of the waters, &c.

Monday, Aug. 30th.—By express train to Paris. (*Hotels St. Petersburg and London and New York.*)

Tuesday, Aug. 31st.   ⎱ **IN PARIS ;** three days to be devoted to carriage drives,
Wednesday, Sept. 1st. ⎰ visiting the principal places of interest in and
Thursday, Sept. 2d.   around the city, including an excursion to St. Cloud,
Friday, Sept. 3d.   Sevres and Versailles, according to programme shown
Saturday, Sept. 4th.   in first section, pages 41-42.
Sunday, Sept. 5th.

Monday, Sept. 6th.—Leave by day service, *via* Rouen, Dieppe and Newhaven, for London. (*Midland Grand Hotel.*)

Passengers who may so desire can leave Paris on Friday evening and spend part of Saturday in Brighton, joining the party again on Saturday evening for London.

Any passenger preferring the short sea mail route, via Calais and Dover, can be supplied with tickets for that route on payment of the difference of fare.

Tuesday, Sept. 7th.—**IN LONDON.**

Wednesday, Sept. 8th.— Proceed by morning express train to **LIVERPOOL,** and spend the remainder of the day visiting the Docks, Royal Exchange and other places of interest. (*Washington Hotel.*)

Thursday, Sept. 9th.—Sail from Liverpool, on steamer "City of Berlin," for Queenstown.

Friday, Sept. 10th.— Arrive at Queenstown, take mails and sail for New York.

Saturday, Sept. 18th.—Expect to arrive at New York.

The Fare for the Second Section includes

First-class Ocean passage both ways,   20 Days.
First-class Hotel accommodations in Great Britain, 7 Days.
First-class Hotel accommodations on the Continent, 23 Days.

Total, 50 Days.

IT ALSO INCLUDES

First-class railway and steamboat traveling for the entire journey; Omnibuses and Porterage between Stations and Hotels; free transportation of 60 lbs. of Baggage; gratuities to Servants; Carriage Excursions to Grindelwald; three days' carriage drives in Paris; fees for sight-seeing, as per Conductor's programme; services of special local guides where necessary, and also the services of the Conductor, who acts as Interpreter and Manager.

NOTE.—*The Conductor will only pay for carriages ordered by himself, and the services of the Guides will be for the whole of the party.*

Hotel provisions for each country to be according to the custom of the country, viz.: in Great Britain, Meat Breakfast, Table d'Hote Dinner, Tea, Bedroom, lights, services and attendance. On the Continent: Meat Breakfast, Dinner at Table d'Hote (with or without wine as the Hotel provides), Bedrooms, lights and service.

THE THIRD SECTION PROVIDES

FOR VISITING

England, France, Switzerland, French Savoy and Italy,

AND INCLUDES

Liverpool, London, Paris, Versailles, Geneva, Chamounix, The Tete Noir, Martigny, Brigue, The Simplon Pass, Verona, Milan, Venice, Bologna, Florence, Rome, Naples, Pompeii, Mt. Vesuvius, Pisa, Genoa, Turin, Paris, Rouen, Dieppe, Newhaven and Brighton.

64 *Days from New York, back to New York, including all necessary expenses.*

Fare, $410.

Itinerary of the Third Section.

Saturday, July 31st.—Leave New York by steamship "City of Richmond" at 1 p. m.

N. B.— We are notified by the Steamship Company that the above-named Steamer is appointed to sail on this date; but we cannot, of course, hold ourselves responsible should any change be made and another Steamer substituted. This, however, is not likely to occur.

Tuesday, Aug. 10th.—Expect to land at Liverpool, and proceed by express train on the Midland Railway to London, going through the celebrated Derbyshire Peak District, and passing Derby, Leicester, Bedford, etc. (*Midland Grand Hotel.*)

Wednesday, Aug. 11th. Thursday, Aug. 12th. Friday, Aug. 13th.	**IN LONDON.** Owing to the great number of places of interest in the Metropolis, and the diversity of opinions as to which places should be visited, no formal programme for sight-seeing will be prepared, but every assistance and information will be afforded to the members of the party by our staff.

Saturday, Aug. 14th.—Leave London for Paris, *via* Newhaven and Dieppe, by 8 p. m. train from London Bridge Station.

Passengers preferring the short Sea Mail Route, via Calais and Dover, can be supplied with tickets for that route on payment of the difference of fare.

Sunday, Aug. 15th.—Arrive in Paris. (*Hotels St. Petersburg and London and New York.*)

Monday, Aug. 16th.
Tuesday, Aug. 17th.
Wednesday, Aug. 18th.
Thursday, Aug. 19th.

IN PARIS, three days of which will be devoted to carriage drives, visiting all the principal places of interest in and around the city, including an excursion to St. Cloud, Sevres and Versailles, according to programme shown in first section, pages 41-42.

Friday, Aug. 20th.—Leave Paris by express train at 8 p. m. for Geneva.

Saturday, Aug. 21st.—Arrive at Geneva. (*Hotels du Lac and de Russie.*)
At Geneva, visits may be made to the Cathedral where Calvin preached, the Russian Church, Rath, Museum, Rousseau's Island, the meeting of the waters, etc.

Sunday, Aug. 22d.—**IN GENEVA.**
Monday, Aug. 23d.—Leave by diligence, *via* Sallanches, for Chamounix. (*Hotel d' Angleterre.*)
Tuesday, Aug. 24th.—**IN THE VALLEY OF CHAMOUNIX.** The hotel here commands a magnificent view of **MONT BLANC**; excursions may be made to the Montanvert, Mauvais Pas, Mer de Glace, Chapeau, Jardin, Flegere, or to the beautiful gorges of **LA DIOZA.**
Wednesday, Aug. 25th.—Go by mules or carriages over the **TETE NOIR** to Martigny. (*Hotel Clerc.*)
Thursday, Aug. 26th.—Leave Martigny by noon train for Brigue, leaving by diligence at 11.40 p. m., through the Simplon Pass, full of picturesque and wild scenery, for Arona.
Friday Aug. 27th.—Arrive at **ARONA** at 6.55 p. m. (*Hotel d' Italie et Poste.*)
Saturday, Aug. 28th.—Travel by morning train to Milan. (*Hotel de Milan.*)
Sunday, Aug. 29th.—**IN MILAN.** The principal sights of Milan are the cathedral, dedicated to Marie Nascenti, one of the finest specimens of Gothic architecture in the world ; the Gallery Vittorio Emanuele or Public Arcade, which is one of the most spacious and attractive of its kind in existence ; the Arch of Peace, the Brera Collection of Pictures and Statues, the Church of Santa Marie delle Grazie, containing, in the Monastery, the celebrated "Last Supper" of Leonardo da Vinci.
Monday, Aug. 30th.—Leave by noon express train for Venice, *via* Brescia, Verona, Padova, etc. Between Desenzano and Peschiera a fine view of the picturesque Lake of Garda is obtained. Reach Venice at 7.10 p. m. (*Hotel Victoria.*)

Tuesday, Aug. 31st.
Wednesday, Sept. 1st.

IN VENICE, during which time gondolas will be provided for visiting the most important points of interest, including the Church of St. Marc, Royal Palace, the Palace of the Doges, the Bridge of Sighs, State Prisons, the principal Churches, Museums, Art Galleries, the Islands of the Lagoons, the Lido, etc. etc.

Thursday, Sept. 2d.—Leave by morning train, *via* Bologna, for Florence. (*Hotels de l' Europe, New York and Russie.*)

Friday, Sept. 3d.—**IN FLORENCE,** visiting the Tombs of the Medicis, the Cathedral and Baptistry, Church of Santa Croce (the Westminster Abbey of Italy), the Uffizi Gallery, Palaces of the Signoria and Pitti, etc., etc.

Saturday, Sept. 4th.—By morning express train, *via* Torontola and Chiusi, to Rome. (*Hotels Allemagne and Continental.*)

Sunday, Sept. 5th.
Monday, Sept. 6th.
Tuesday, Sept. 7th.
Wednesday, Sept. 8th.

IN ROME, three days of which will be devoted to carriage excursions, under the superintendence of Mr. Shakspere Wood, the eminent archæologist, according to the following programme :

FIRST DAY.

THE PALATINE.—The Seven Hills ; remains of the Walls of Romulus and Port Mugonia ; remains of Temples and Edifices of the early Republic ; remains of

Houses of the Republican period ; House of Tiberius Claudius Nero, with Fresco paintings,

THE PALACE OF THE CÆSARS.—Site of the House of Augustus ; Palace of Tiberius ; substructions of the Palace of Caligula, and Porticos built by him to the Domus Tiberiana : great suite of State rooms built by Domitian ; Lararium, Basilica, Triclinium, etc. ; Intermontium ; great Stadium of Domitian ; gigantic Porticos of Septimus Severus ; site of Septizonium, etc., etc.

BASILICA OF CONSTANTINE.

ARCH OF TITUS.—Bas-relief of Soldiers carrying Seven-branched Candlestick, etc.

(AFTER LUNCH.)

THE COLOSSEUM.	THE PANTHEON.
TEMPLE OF VENUS AND ROME.	TEMPLE OF FORTUNA VIRILIS.
REMAINS OF DOMUS TRANSITORIA OF NERO.	PONTE ROTTO and View along the Tiber. THE CLOACA MAXIMA.
ARCH OF CONSTANTINE.	THEATRE OF MARCELLUS.
META SUDANS.	THE PORTICO OF OCTAVIA.
TEMPLE OF VESTA.	

SECOND DAY.

THE FORUM ROMANUM.—Via Sacra ; Vicus Tuscus ; Clivus Capitolinus ; Temples of Castor and Pollux, the Deified Julius, Saturn, Vespasian, Concord ; the Basilica Julia ; Honorary Monuments, the Pedestal of Domitian's Statue, Column of Phocas ; Rostrum ; Arch of Septimus Severus ; Portico of the Deii Consentes ; the Tabularium.

THE TARPEIAN ROCK.

THE MAMERTINE PRISON.

THE FORA OF THE EMPERORS Augustus, Nerva, Trajan.

(AFTER LUNCH.)

THE GOLDEN HOUSE OF NERO.

BATHS OF TITUS.

BASILICA OF ST. CLEMENT ; the Basilica of the Twelfth Century ; the now subterranean Basilica of the Fourth Century ; marvelously preserved Frescoes ; House of Clement ; Temple of Mithras ; remains of a grand edifice of the Republican period, superimposed on a portion of the wall of the Kings, beneath the subterranean Basilica.

BASILICA OF ST. JOHN LATERAN.

THE SCALA SANCTA.

AQUEDUCT OF NERO.

BASILICA OF ST. PAUL, Outside the Walls.

THIRD DAY.

VATICAN MUSEUM OF SCULPTURE.

THE SIXTINE CHAPEL.—Michael Angelo's "Last Judgment."

STANZE AND LOGGIE OF RAPHAEL.

VATICAN PICTURE GALLERY.—"The Transfiguration ;" "Communion of St. Jerome ;" "Madonna di Foligno," &c., &c.

(AFTER LUNCH.)

BATHS OF CARACALLA ; PORTA ST. SEBASTIANO ; COLOMBARIA.

THE APPIAN WAY.—Tombs of Geta, Priscilla, Cecilia Metella, Seneca, the Cotta Family, &c., &c. ; Tumuli of the Horatii and Curiatii ; the Villa of the Quintilii; the Ustrinum ; the Circus of Romulus ; the Catacombs. (See "Cook's New Guide to Ancient and Modern Rome," price $2.00.)

Thursday, Sept. 9th.—Leave by morning train for Naples. (Hotels de Russie and Metropole.)

Friday, Sept. 10th.
Saturday, Sept. 11th.
Sunday, Sept. 12th.

IN NAPLES, during which time the party will visit the principal places of interest in the city and surroundings, including carriage drives to Pompeii and Vesuvius.

Monday, Sept. 13th.—By convenient train to Rome. (*Hotels d'Allemagne and Continental.*)

Tuesday, Sept. 14th.—Leave at 2.30 p. m. for **PISA.** (*Hotel de Londres.*)

Wednesday, Sept. 15th.—The morning will be spent in viewing the Cathedral, Baptistry, Leaning Tower, Campo Santo, etc., leaving by noon train by the new Riviera Railway for Genoa. (*Hotel de la Ville.*)

Thursday, Sept. 16th.— **IN GENOA,** visiting the Cathedral, Church of the Annunziata, Palace of the Doges, Public Gardens, etc.

Friday, Sept. 17th.— Leave at 7.40 a. m. for **TURIN.** (*Hotels Trombetta and d'Angleterre.*) The remainder of the day may be spent in visiting the Royal Palace, Museums, Cathedral, Squares, etc.

Saturday, Sept. 18th.—Leave by express train at 9 a. m. for Paris.

Sunday, Sept. 19th.—Arrive **IN PARIS.** (*Hotels St. Petersburg* and *London and New York, etc.*)

Monday, Sept. 20th.—Leave Paris by day service, *via* Rouen, Dieppe and Newhaven, for London. (*Midland Grand Hotel.*)

Passengers who may so desire can leave Paris on Friday evening and spend part of Saturday in Brighton, joining the party again on Saturday evening for London.

Tuesday, Sept. 21st.—**IN LONDON.**

Wednesday, Sept. 22d.— Proceed by morning express train to **LIVERPOOL,** and spend the remainder of the day visiting the Docks, Royal Exchange, and other places of interest. (*Washington Hotel.*)

Thursday, Sept. 23d.—Sail from Liverpool on the steamship "City of Richmond" for Queenstown.

Friday, Sept. 24th.—Arrive at Queenstown, take the mails and sail for New York.

Saturday, Oct. 2d.—Expect to arrive at New York.

The Tour for the Third Section includes

First-class Ocean passage both ways,   20 Days.
First-class Hotel accommodations in Great Britain,   8 Days.
First-class Hotel accommodations on the Continent,   36 Days.

Total, 64 Days.

IT ALSO INCLUDES

First-class railway and steamboat traveling for the entire journey; Omnibuses and Porterage between Stations and Hotels; free transportation of 60 lbs. of Baggage; gratuities to servants; three days' carriage drives in Paris; three days' carriages in Rome, and services of Mr. Shakspere Wood; trip to Pompeii; one day's gondolas in Venice; fees for sight-seeing, as per Conductor's programme; services of special local guides where necessary and also the services of the Conductor, who acts as Interpreter and Manager.

NOTE.—*The Conductor will only pay for carriages ordered by himself, and the services of the Guides will be for the whole of the party.*

Hotel provision for each country to be according to the custom of the country, viz.: in Great Britain, Meat Breakfast, Table d'Hote Dinner, Tea, Bedroom, lights, services, and attendance. On the Continent: Meat breakfast, Dinner at Table d'Hote, (with or without wine as the Hotel provides), Bedrooms, lights and service.

A Deposit of Fifty Dollars

Is required from each person who decides to go with either of the sections of this tour. When the deposit is made, the name is registered, and the berths are allotted in the exact order of these deposits, the earliest depositors, of course, receiving the best berths.

Forty dollars of this deposit may be withdrawn up to July 12th, after which time the whole amount is due.

How to Join the Party.

Persons desirous of joining this party should write us as early as possible, enclosing draft on any bank, or postal order, made payable to the order of THOS. COOK & SON, *and stating distinctly which section they wish to join.* We will, upon receipt of the same, return a "Deposit Receipt" and a plan of the steamer, showing the location of the berths we can offer. Should the choice of berths be left to us, we will use our best judgment in the interest of each, and advise them at once. The balance of the money can be paid any time after July 12th.

The Staterooms

Are all on the main deck, and are arranged for two and three persons ; the two-berth rooms are for married couples, thus accommodating family parties and friends. Berths are allotted in accordance with the order in which passengers book.

Extension of Time.

The steamship tickets for these tours are good to return any time during the year on any steamer of the Inman Line which sails from Liverpool or Queenstown.

BREAKS IN THE JOURNEY can be made at almost any principal point, and as the return steamship tickets are good for one year, any of the members of this party can remain in Europe at their discretion The whole of the fare must be paid before starting, but they can receive back the value of their unused tickets and hotel coupons, less 10 per cent., (*Swiss traveling tickets excepted,*) at the Chief London Office, or they can be exchanged for tickets to other points at their full value.

On the return from the Continent, if any wish to extend their tour to the English Lakes, Scotland and Ireland, taking the steamer at Liverpool or Queenstown, quotations will be given by Messrs. Thos. Cook & Son; and if a party of ten or more be made up for this supplementary tour, a conductor will be sent with them without extra charge.

A very interesting tour from London, combining the English Lakes, Melrose, Abbotsford, Edinburgh, Stirling, the Trossachs, Loch Lomond, Loch Katrine, Glasgow, Belfast, the Giant's Causeway, Dublin, and the Lakes of Killarney, thence to Queenstown to join the steamer, may be accomplished comfortably in from ten to twelve days. Passengers who have made up their minds to make the above tour, after they have visited the Continent, can have a quotation from the New York office for the entire fare.

Other Lines of Steamers.

To any who desire to avail themselves of this Tour and join this party, but prefer some other line of steamers, we can accommodate them, and will give them a special quotation either higher or lower, according to the line preferred. We will also, for those who have engaged steamship passage, give quotations, and book them from Liverpool, London or Paris.

Detours.

Any member of the above party will be allowed to leave the main party to visit other localities, provided he gives early notice to the Conductor, so engagements for hotel accommodations may not be violated.

Hotel coupons will be supplied those who so leave the party, for the number of days they expect to be absent. Any unused coupons to be redeemed at the advertised rate.

LETTERS may be addressed to any member of the party, care of THOMAS COOK & SON, LUDGATE CIRCUS, LONDON, and such letters will be carefully forwarded to the Conductor of the party for delivery.

MONEY, LETTERS OF CREDIT AND CIRCULAR CHECKS are issued by us, at current rates, in the denomination of five or ten pounds sterling each, and are payable at nearly every point on the route, or will be cashed by the Conductor as required, and in the currency of the country where the party happens to be at the time.

Cautionary Proviso, applying to all Sections.

The liability of Alpine roads and railroads in the neighborhood of mountains to damage from storms and other influences beyond human control, renders it necessary that we should announce that we cannot be responsible for detention or expenses incurred by deviation of routes occasioned by circumstances of this nature; nor for delays or deviation that may be caused through the railway being required for military purposes.

The most that companies will do under such circumstances is to repay the value of any tickets or proportion of tickets not used for lines thus rendered impassable ; and all claims in such cases must be sent in writing, accompanied by the unused tickets, within one month from the date for which such tickets were available.

BAGGAGE.—Whilst anxious to render all possible assistance to the travelers in the transport, care and registration of baggage, THOS. COOK & SON cannot admit responsibility in cases of detention, stray conveyance, damage to or loss of baggage. In all cases of transference it is necessary that baggage should be identified by its owners, especially on entering and leaving hotels and railway stations; and whenever baggage is subject to Customs examination its owner should be present to answer for it.

N. B.—Great care will be taken in the registration and conveyance of the trunks or portmanteaus of the parties whilst traveling with the Conductor; but it must be distinctly understood that all small packages, such as handbags, umbrellas, traveling rugs, &c., must remain entirely under the control of the passenger.

THOS. COOK & SON,
261 BROADWAY, NEW YORK.

USEFUL HINTS FOR TOURISTS, CONCERNING EUROPEAN TRAVEL.

Passports.—As a rule, passports are unnecessary for the countries these parties will visit ; still, if war should break out, passports might be needed. It only requires three days to get them from the State Department, and we will procure them for 50 cents each, in addition to the Government fee of $5. Applicants must fill up a blank, and swear to it before a notary, whose seal must be attached. The proper way to get them is to send us 50 cents for the blank, fill the blank up, have it properly attested by a notary, and return it to us with $5 enclosed. There are two kinds of blanks—one for native born, and the other for naturalized citizens. Naturalized citizens must send their naturalization papers with their application, and the papers will be returned with the passport.

Baggage.—It is of the greatest importance that passengers should take as little baggage with them on their tour as possible, as high rates are charged for extra baggage, especially on the Continent, and the limited weight allowed to tourists is 100 pounds on ocean steamers and up to London, 66 pounds being the weight allowed on the Continent of Europe. A strong medium-sized wooden or leather trunk is preferable, and where friends are traveling together, or in the case of married couples, a single trunk may serve for two persons. A small hand-bag or satchel, together with a shawl-strap, will be found of great convenience. Travelers should avoid overloading themselves with unnecessary bundles and packages. A most valuable and useful article is a small field or large opera-glass, which should have a strap attached, by which it can be carried over the shoulder.

A strong umbrella is frequently useful as a protection against sun and rain.

SPECIAL NOTE TO BE OBSERVED ABOUT BAGGAGE.

When leaving any hotel immediately after breakfast, to make a journey to another city, the trunks and small hand-bags should be packed, locked and strapped before leaving the bed-room. While at breakfast, the porters will remove all baggage, placing the small articles where you can lay your hands on them before entering the omnibus, and convey the large baggage to the station.

Clothing.—For the ocean passage, the tourist should provide himself for all kinds of weather. The clothing should be ample, to guard against chills, and outside wraps, shawls, overcoats, worsted leggins and rugs will be found highly useful. Ladies will find camel-hair serge or woolen dresses the best. Jewelry of value should not be taken, with the exception, perhaps, of one set, to be worn constantly. Gentlemen will find warm clothing throughout, with an overcoat, very serviceable, so that prolonged sojourns may be made upon the deck, and cold winds may be encountered without discomfort. All clothing worn on steamers may be left behind either at Glasgow, Liverpool, or at our Chief Office, Ludgate Circus, London, where it will be stored at a slight expense. For traveling on the Continent, ladies should have a traveling and walking dress, and a black silk or stylish costume for receptions or dress occasions. For gentlemen, a traveling suit, also a black suit for dress occasions. If a full-dress suit is found necessary, it may be hired at a slight expense at almost every place.

Washing.—In hotels on the Continent of Europe there are ample facilities for getting washing for travelers done quickly. It should be given to the chambermaid early in the day, and a list made out of the articles, with the day and hour at which they are required to be returned clearly written at the foot.

Washing books, in different languages, may be obtained at any of Cook's Tourist Offices.

Sundries.—A few suggestions as to some further requisites may be appreciated. A pocket compass will be found invaluable; a light scrap-book, and of a size easily disposed of in packing; a package or two of address or visiting cards; toilet soap; case with needles, thread, ball of string, buttons, scissors, penknife, and such other little articles as may suggest themselves and which may prove useful.

Medicines.—It is not our vocation to prescribe, but aperient or astringent medicines may be required, and quinine is not unfrequently of use. Parties would do well to consult their usual medical attendant on this subject before leaving. First-class physicians and apothecaries can be found in all principal cities in Europe, and usually in our parties there is some member of the medical profession. A little court plaster, extract of ginger, ammonia, arnica, or some kind of liniment, enter into every tourist's outfit.

Foreign Moneys.—On page 53 of this pamphlet will be found an explanation of our Circular Notes and Letters of Credit and of our Foreign Banking and Exchange Department ; and on 3d page of cover we also give a money table showing the relative value of European currencies.

Custom House Examinations.—All baggage is examined by the Custom House authorities in the various countries visited by these parties, and every assistance will be rendered by our conductors to facilitate this matter. Travelers should be in readiness with their keys and answer correctly, stating the contents of any trunks or parcels, and give to the officials every aid in the performance of their duty.

Languages.—Whilst a knowledge of some of the Continental languages is very useful, still persons traveling with our parties do not absolutely need to speak them, as the conductor acts as interpreter where necessary, and English is spoken by almost all of the hotel keepers, waiters and merchants throughout the Continent.

The traveler will do well to provide himself with a copy of the "Tourist's Conversational Guide to France, Germany and Italy," by J. T. Loth, which can be obtained at any of our offices, price 35 cents.

Guide Books and Maps—A list of our Guide Books is shown on 2d page of cover.

Circular Notes and Letters of Credit

Six years ago we commenced a system of Circular Notes for the accommodation of our travelers. These Notes are of the value of £5 or £10 each, and can be purchased at the Chief American Office, 261 Broadway, New York, or at our Chief Office, Ludgate Circus, London.

In addition to all the conveniences of ordinary Circular Notes, they have the advantage of being, by our special arrangements, cashed at all the Hotels on our list, and also by the Conductors of our parties. By this system passengers obviate the delays which frequently arise to travelers who, arriving at certain points on the Continent after banking hours, and who only wish to stay the one night, and would leave early the next morning but for the fact that they must lose a day or a portion of a day through having to wait for the opening of the bank.

These Notes have been issued in such large numbers during the past few years, that we felt justified, in 1878, in making

FOREIGN BANKING AND EXCHANGE

a special department of our business, at our Chief Office in London, where travelers from America can receive, in exchange for their Circular Notes, obtained at our New York Office, current coin of the various countries they intend to pass through during their tour in Europe. The Circular Notes are all made payable to the order of the holder, and are of no value without bearing the holder's signature.

Cook's International Reading and Waiting Rooms,

at Ludgate Circus and 445 Strand, London, are open for the free use of all travelers, or parties, with Cook's Tickets.

BAGGAGE STORED in London at either Ludgate Circus or 445 Strand, or forwarded to any part of the globe.

BRIEF DESCRIPTIONS

OF THE

PRINCIPAL CITIES AND PLACES IN EUROPE

VISITED BY

COOK'S

Personally Conducted Parties from America.

AMSTERDAM (Holland).—Pop. 280,000. Built on a number of islands, intersected by canals. Places of interest :—Trippenhuis Museum of Paintings, 10 to 3 : New Church, Palace. Museum van der Hoop, Old Church, Zoological Gardens, etc.

ANTWERP (Belgium).—Pop. 130,000. Situated on the River Scheldt, which is navigable for large vessels. Places of interest :—Cathedral, with Rubens' "Descent from the Cross," "Elevation of the Cross," etc.; Church of St. Paul ; Hotel de Ville ; Museum ; Church of St. Jacques : Church of the Augustines; Church of St. Andrew; Iron Pump Head, by Quintin Matsys.

BADEN BADEN (Grand Duchy of Baden).—Pop. 10,000. Prettily situated on the borders of the Black Forest, into which many interesting carriage excursions may be made. Places of interest:—Kursaal; Neue Schloss; Alte Schloss, etc.

BALE (Switzerland).—Pop. 45,000. On the Rhine, at the north-west corner of Switzerland. Places of interest:—Cathedral, with Council Hall: Museum; Hotel de Ville; Battle-field of St. Jacob, ¼ mile; Battle-field of Dornach, 2 miles.

BRUSSELS (Belgium).—Pop. 262,000. This city, the capital of the Kingdom and the seat of Government, is 88 miles from Ostend, 27½ from Antwerp, 48 from Ghent, 71¼ from Liege, 92¼ from Lille, 149¼ from Cologne, and 215 from Paris. Places of interest : Cathedral of St. Gudule; Galeries St. Hubert; Hotel de Ville; Museum; Royal Palace; Palace of the Duke of Arenberg; Musée Wiertz; Park; Zoological Gardens, etc. The Field of Waterloo is 12 miles from Brussels. (Cook's Tourist Office, 22 Galerie du Roi.)

BERNE (Switzerland).—Pop. 37,000. The capital of the Canton Berne, and seat of Swiss Government. Situated on the River Aar, which nearly encircles the city. Places of interest:—Cathedral, with Domplatz: Federal Palace; Museum: Clock Tower: Rathhaus; Roman Catholic Church, etc., etc.

CHAMOUNY (Savoy).—3,150 feet above the level of the sea. A village in the valley of the same name, at the foot of Mont Blanc, distant about 50 miles from Geneva. Diligences in the season. Distance from Martigny to Chamounix, 22 miles. Several days may be well devoted to explore this celebrated region.

The Montanvert, which can be ascended on mules, and commands a view of the Mer de Glace, ought to be the first excursion. It is an elevated pasture on the summit of a mountain under the Aiguilles de Charmoz. From this are seen to advantage the heights of the Brevent and of the Aiguilles Rouges. At the summit of the Montanvert is a small building, where beds and refreshments may be had. The height of Montanvert above the valley of Chamounix is 2,565 feet. The Glacier de Bossons, which may be seen the same day, at the other end of the valley, is remarkable for the purity of the ice, and for the picturesque formation of its ice needles and obelisks. The Brevent, on the opposite side of the valley, 8,000 feet above the sea, affords a magnificent view of the whole range of Mont Blanc, with its numerous peaks covered with snow, and the glaciers pouring down into the valley. The Flegere, on the same side, commands the same view at a less elevation, and may be accomplished in half a day. The active mountaineer would be well repaid by a day's excursion to the Jardin, across the Mer de Glace, 9,100 feet above the sea—a small portion of green earth, covered with flowers in full bloom, in a region of snow and ice, commanding a view of the recesses of this wonderful range of snowy peaks. From Chamounix to Martigny, by the passes of the Tete Noire or the Col de Balme, about nine hours would be required; these roads are practicable for mules. To the Jardin is a fatiguing and severe excursion for ladies. They are sometimes deceived by guides, who take them to another spot. The Tete Noire is one of the most picturesque passes in Switzerland, the rocks frequently overhanging.

COLOGNE (Germany).—This, the chief city of Rhenish Prussia, contains a population of 130,000. It is strongly fortified, and is connected with its suburb Deutz by two bridges; one a handsome iron structure, and the other, 1,250 feet in length, composed of 39 boats. The chief objects of attraction are: the Cathedral, which, when finally completed, will probably be the finest specimen of Gothic architecture in the world. Nave and transept free; fee to see the choir (free only from 8½—9 a. m.), the relics of the three Kings, and the treasury, 15 sgr.; to ascend the tower and galleries, 10 sgr.; Churches of St. Martin, St. Maria in Capitolio, St. Peter's (containing the "Crucifixion of Peter," by Rubens), St. Ursula (where the relics of the Eleven Thousand Virgins are to be seen in the walls; fee, 15 sgr). English Chapel, Templehans, 8, Rheingasse, Rev. E. H. F. Hartman, D. D. Services: Sunday morning, 11; evening (summer months), 6. Cook's Tourist Office, 40 Domhof.

DIEPPE (France). Pop. 26,000. A prettily-situated watering place in Normandy. Places of interest:—Church of St. Jacques; Church of St. Remi; the Plage or Promenade overlooking the sea; the Chateau d'Arques, 3 miles. etc.

FLORENCE (Italy).—Pop. 168,000. Beautifully situated on both sides of the Arno. Places of interest:—Cathedral, with Giotto's Campanile, Brunelleschi's Cupola and the Baptistry with Ghiberti's bronze doors; Churches of Santa Annunziata; Il Carmine; Santa Croce; San Lorenzo; Laurent de Medicis: San Marco; Santa Maria Novella; San Michele, etc. The Uffizi and Pitti palaces, connected by a covered way, containing the richest collection of paintings and sculptures in the world; the Palazzo Vecchio; the Palazzo Riccardi, etc.; also the Galleria Reale; the Academy of Fine Arts; the Houses of Michael Angelo, Dante, Galileo, etc. Modern Paintings:—Societa Artistica, Viale Principe Eugenio. R. W. Spranger, Managing Director.

FRANKFORT (Germany).— Pop. 106,000. Formerly a free city, and the seat of the German Bund. Situated on the River Main, which is spanned by five bridges. Places of interest:—Town Hall; Gutenberg Monument; statues of Schiller and Goethe; Cathedral; Town Library; Gallery of Paintings; Stadel Art Institution; Leuckenberg Museum and Library; Bethmann Museum; Natural History Museum; Palmengarten; Exchange, etc.

FREIBURG (Baden.)— Pop. 22,000. Situated on the River Dreisam, at the entrance to the Hollenthal (Black Forest). Places of interest:—The Cathedral or

Minster; the Archbishop's Palace; and the Palace of the Grand Duke; Kaufhaus, etc. Freiburg is a convenient centre for excursions into the Black Forest.

FRIBOURG (Switzerland).—Pop. 11,000. Beautifully situated on the side of a deep gorge. Places of interest:—Cathedral with famous organ, 70 stops, 7,800 pipes, generally played at noon, also a bas-relief over the entrance; great suspension bridge, 964 feet long, 186 feet high; small suspension bridge, 746 feet long, 303 feet high; Lime-tree of Fribourg opposite the ancient Rathhaus.

GENEVA (Switzerland).—Pop. 56,000. Situated at the point where the River Rhone issues from the Lake; 370 miles from Paris. Places of interest:— Bridge and Quai of Mont Blanc; Jardin Anglais; Isle Jean Jacques Rousseau; Tour de César; Musée Rath; Conservatoire de Musique; Hotel de Ville; Cathedral where Calvin preached; Russian Chapel; Library, etc. Cook's Tourist Office, 90 Rue du Rhône.

GENOA (Italy).—Pop. 140,000. One of the chief ports of Italy. Streets lined with marble palaces. Cathedral of San Lorenzo very fine. Church of Annunziata. Best view of the town obtained from the Tower of Santa Maria di Carignano. Before ascending it is best to tell the Sacristan how many minutes you intend to remain, so that on descending he may open the door. The Campo Santo contains many fine monuments.

HAGUE (Holland).—Pop. 80,000. This has the reputation of being the "largest village in the world." It is the residence of the Court. Places of interest:—Palace in the Wood; Museum of medals; Museum of paintings; Bittenhof; Buitenhof; Scheveningen, a fashionable bathing place, is four miles distant.

HEIDELBERG (Baden).—Pop. 20,000. Situated on the River Neckar. The magnificent ruins of the Castle, one of the most interesting objects in Europe, occupy the hill behind the town. In a cellar under the castle is the celebrated "Tun of Heidelberg." The University is attended by about 500 students. Many charming excursions may be made in the neighborhood.

INTERLAKEN (Switzerland).—Situated in the Canton Berne, this little town forms the chief centre for excursions into the Bernese Oberland. The hotels are for the most part very fine. Berne is reached by railway as far as Darligen, thence by steamer to Scherzligen-Thun, and forward by railway; Lucerne is reached by railway to Bonigen, steamer to Brienz, past the celebrated Giessbach falls, diligence over the Brunig pass to Alpnach, and thence by steamer. Grindelwald, 12 miles from Interlaken and Lauterbrunnum, where is the Staubbach waterfall, may be easily reached by carriage. The Kursaal of Interlaken is one of the best in the country.

LONDON (England). It is impossible to give a description of such a large city as London in this connection, but it may be here briefly stated that the population of the great Metropolis is between four and five millions, and that it is the largest and most important commercial city in the world. The principal places of interest are:—St. Paul's Cathedral; Westminster Abbey; the Tower of London; the Houses of Parliament; British Museum: Royal Exchange; Mansion House; Bank of England, etc., etc. For a description of these and other places of interest, and also for information as to how to get round the city and economize time, the traveler would do well to consult "Cook's Handbook to London;" but a more elaborate description will be found in Baedeker's Guide to London.

LAUSANNE (Switzerland).— Pop. 27,000. Situated on the northern bank of the Lake of Geneva. The Cathedral is the grandest Gothic structure in Switzerland. Vevey, Clarens, Castle of Chillon, Vernex, Montreux. etc., on the eastern shore of the Lake, may be easily visited from Ouchy, which is the port of Lausanne. A railway worked by hydraulic power connects Lausanne with Ouchy.

LUCERNE (Switzerland).—Pop. 14,000. Situated on the Lake and the River Reuss, commanding views of the Alps, including the Righi, Pilatus, etc. Places of interest: Cathedral, Thorwaldsen's Lion; Glacier Garden; Stauffer's Museum; Covered Bridges; old Roman watch-tower; Arsenal, etc. Steamers ply frequently between all the points of interest on the Lake.

MILAN (Italy).—Pop. 270,000. A convenient centre for tours in the Italian Lake district. Places of interest:—The Cathedral, the largest marble structure in the world (fine view from top of tower); Churches of St. Alessandro, St. Ambrogio, St. Maria delle Grazie, near which is the celebrated painting of "The Last Supper," by Leonardo da Vinci; La Scala Theatre; Royal Palace; Brera; Arch of Peace, &c.

MUNICH (Bavaria)—(pop. 170,000)—capital of Bavaria, is the headquarters of modern German art, and one of the most beautiful towns of Germany. There are several very fine churches; the Basilica of St. Boniface, in the Carlstrasse, is, without exception, the most beautiful church in Germany, in the Byzantine style. The Royal Palace consists of two parts, the old and new, a beautiful edifice after the model of the Pitti Palace in Florence, and rich in fresco paintings. The Colossal Statue of Bavaria and her Lion, half a mile from the Sendlinger Thor, is of copper, upwards of 60 feet high, on a pedestal of marble 40 feet high. A spiral staircase leads to the top; the head will hold eight persons, and there are holes to enable them to view the surrounding country. The Royal Library, a superb edifice in the Ludwig Strasse, with room enough to hold two millions of volumes, and in richness the second in the world; its Reading Room is open Monday, Wednesday, and Friday, from 8 to 1 o'clock. The traveler should refer to the small daily German newspaper called the "Taglisher Anzeiger," for all particulars relating to the Public Exhibitions and Amusements at Munich.

NAPLES (Italy). Pop. 500,000. Situated in latitude 40° 52′; has a mean temperature of 60°–63° Fahr., the extreme heat of summer rarely attaining to 100°, and the extreme cold in winter 28°. There are five principal entrances; that by the bridge Della Maddalena near the Bay is the most striking; most of the houses are lofty and the streets narrow; there are, however, several open spaces of squares. The number of churches at Naples is about 330, and those best worth a visit are Gesu Nuovo, in the style of St. Peter's at Rome; the Sans Severo, a private chapel (remarkable statuary), San Francesco da Paolo; the Cathedral and the San Martino; St. Domenico Maggiore, San Severino e Soggia; La Incoronata; San Filippo Neri; San Lorenzo Maggiore; St. Maria del Carmine; all of them being adorned with pictures, &c., of the first masters. The National Museum will repay a good many visits, it possessing besides a picture gallery, the fresco paintings, mosaics, gold and silver ornaments, etruscan vases, &c., discovered in the excavations of Pompeii and Herculaneum. The Royal Library is annexed to the National Museum, and contains 250,000 volumes, besides more than 1,700 papyri, found in Herculaneum. The Albergo dei Poveri, an establishment for paupers and orphans, is worthy of a visit. It affords fixed relief to about 5,000 poor, and pays the debts of deserving individuals. The environs abound with beauty and delightful reminiscences, including Virgil's Tomb, the Grotto of Posilippo, the Ruins of Pozzuoli, Lake Avernus, and the classic shores of Baia and Misenum, the Islands of Ischia, Procida and Capri; the coast to Castellamare, the Orange Groves of Sorrento, Vesuvius, and the fields of lava; the streets of Pompeii, and the excavations of Herculaneum. The ascent of Vesuvius occupies about 8 hours; it is advisable to take refreshments with you, and to ride as far as the horses can go. Punta del Nasone, on Monte Somma, is 3,747 feet above the sea, but the highest point, Punta del Palo, is nearly 4,000 feet. The ruins of Paestum may be visited in a day. Another delightful excursion is by railway to Castellamare (1 hour), and from thence to Sorrento, by carriage along the side of the Bay, one of the most beautiful drives in the world. English Church, Strada San Pasquale, at the back of the Riviera di Chiaja; the Rev. Pelham Maitland, M. A., is chaplain. Presbyterian church, 5, Capella Vecchia; Minister, Rev. James Gordon Grey. Italian Evangelical Church and Schools, Palazzo Barbaia, No. 210, Toledo; Pastor, Rev. T. W. S. Jones, Wesleyan Missionary.

PARIS.—The capital of France. Pop. last census, 1,884,874. The principal public buildings and places of interest, with the hours at which they are open, are as follows:—

MUSEUMS.—The Louvre, every day except Monday, 10 a. m. to 4 p. m. Luxemburg, Sundays, 2 to 4 p. m.; other days, except Monday, on production of passport, 11 a. m. to 4 p. m. Cluny (Boulevard St. Michel), daily on production of passport. Artillery Museum of the Invalides, Tuesday. Thursday and Sunday, 12 noon to 3 p. m. Depuytre (Ecole de Medicine), daily to students and medical men. Medailles (National Library), Tuesday, 11 a. m. to 3 p. m. Mineralogique (Boulevard St. Michel), Tuesday, Thursday and Saturday, 11 a. m. to 4 p. m. Museum of the Jardin des Plantes, Tuesday, Thursday and Saturday, by ticket.

CHURCHES.—La Madeleine, Notre Dame, St. Augustine, St. Eustache, St. Severin, St. Germain l'Auxerrois, St. Sulpice, St. Vincent de Paul, Larbonne, Chapelle Expiatoire de Louis XVI., all open daily; Saint Chapelle, open daily, except Friday and Monday.

REMARKABLE BUILDINGS.—Hotel des Invalides, daily, 12 to 3. Tomb of Napoleon, Monday, Tuesday, Thursday, and Friday, 12 noon to 3 p. m. Hotel Dieu (Notre Dame), Thursday and Sunday; Tour St. Jacques, daily; Porte St. Denis; Porte St. Martin; Pantheon, daily; Prisons of Mazas and La Roquette, by order of the Prefect of Police; Institute de France, daily, except Sundays; Imprimerie Nationale, by order of the Director; National Library, daily, except Sunday; Mazarine Library, daily, from September to July; Ste. Genevieve Library, daily; National Archives, daily, except Sunday, 11 to 3; Bourse, daily, except Sunday; Gobelins, Wednesday and Saturday during summer; College de France, daily; Conservatoire des Arts, free on Sunday and Thursday, other days 1 franc.

THE PRINCIPAL STREETS AND THOROUGHFARES IN PARIS are the Champs Elysee, leading from the Tuileries Gardens to the Arc de Triomphe, which was built by Napoleon at a cost of £418,000; Bois de Boulogne, a public park laid out with great skill; Champ de Mars, a large open space facing the Military School.

THE PRINCIPAL BOULEVARDS are the Capucines, des Italiens, Montmartre, Poissonnier, St. Denis, St. Martin, du Prince Regent, Temple, Sebastopol and Strasbourg. The Rue de Rivoli and the Rue St. Honore are the main thoroughfares of the centre of the city.

PARIS is surrounded by fortifications 34,000 yards long. The city contains about 63,000 houses, 80 open spaces or squares, 27 bridges over the River Seine, 75 churches, 13 palaces, 35 theatres, 18 asylums or hospitals, 8 large public libraries, 6 lycees, and upwards of 2,000 schools and educational institutions.

The principal places of interest in the suburbs of Paris are: St. Cloud (5 miles), reached by tram, railway, or steamer. St. Denis, where is the celebrated abbey church of St. Denis. Versailles (15 miles)—here is the magnificent Palace erected by Louis XIV. at a cost of £40,000,000. Sevres, the Government Porcelain Manufactory; St. Germain en Laye, with some very pretty country scenery; Fontainbleau (Forest and Park), 2 hours by rail, 16 trains a day.

PISA (Italy).—Pop. 26,000. One of the most ancient and beautiful cities of Italy. Situated on the Arno. The chief places of interest besides the Cathedral, Baptistry, Leaning Tower and Campo Santo, are the church of St. Stephen, in which are the remains of ships taken from the Turks in the 10th century, and more than 300 flags taken in Palestine in the 9th and 10th centuries; the Pine Forests, 40 miles by 10, extending from Pisa to the sea, and stocked with every kind of selected game, as deer, wild boar, and pheasants. (Here there are a number of camels employed as beasts of burden.) Near Pisa (Viareggio) the poet Shelley was drowned. The interior of the Chartreuse, three-quarters of an

hour from Pisa, is rich in pictures, marbles, and gardens. Half an hour's walk
through a fine avenue of trees brings the visitor to the Spring of San Giuliano,
esteemed by the Romans for its medicinal qualities. In addition, there are in
or near Pisa, the churches of St. Catharine, S. Rattori, the Cascine S. Rossore,
and Gombo, a small bathing place. Lucca is half an hour and Leghorn twenty
minutes by rail from Pisa.

ROME (the Capital of Italy)—(pop. 245,000)—is situated on the Tiber,
partly on a plain and partly on low hills with their intersecting valleys, about 16
miles from the mouth of the river. Walls of 15 miles in circuit surround the
entire city. The modern city is built upon the Campus Martius of the ancient
Romans, lying along the banks of the Tiber, to the north of the seven hills,
which formed the site of ancient Rome. There are 364 Churches; the principal
ones are as follows:—St. Peter's, St. John Lateran, Santa Maria Maggiore, and
Santa Croce in Gerusalemme, within the city: St. Paolo, San Lorenzo, and San
Sebastian; the largest, St. Peter's, is built in form of a Latin cross. It occupied
a period of 176 years in building, and required 350 years to perfect it, and cost
£10,000,000; being kept in repair at a cost of £6,300 per annum. St. John Lateran
is the Pope's Metropolitan church, he being its official minister. It is in this
church also that the Popes were crowned. The Vatican stands prominent amongst
the Palaces here, and is the Winter Palace of the Pope, and stands over the Vatican
Hill, near to St. Peter's. Here are also the Sixtine Chapel, and Vatican Library,
containing the richest collection of manuscripts and pictures in the world. List
of principal places and objects of interest in Rome: The Palatine with Palace of
the Cæsars; Basilica of Constantine; Arch of Titus; Temple of Venus and Rome;
Domus Transitorio of Nero; Arch of Constantine; Meta Sudans; Colosseum;
Lateran Museums; Basilica of St. John Lateran; Scala Sancta; Aqueduct of Nero;
Church of St. Stefano Rotonda; Temple of Vesta; Temple of Fortuna Virilis;
Cloaca Maxima; Temples of Juno, Hope, and Piety; Theatre of Marcellus, Por-
tico of Octavia; Forum Romanum; Mamertine Prison; Capitoline Museums;
Tarpeian Rock; Fora of Trajan, Augustus, and Nerva; Golden House of Nero and
Baths of Titus; Basilica of St. Clement; Basilica of St. Maria Maggiore; Church
of Sta Pudenziana; Vatican Museums; Sixtine Chapel; Stanze and Loggie of
Raphael; Vatican Picture Gallery; St. Peter's, with ascent of Dome; he Pan-
theon; Basilica of Antoninus Pius; Antonine column; Janus Quadrifrons; Gold-
smith's Arch; Circus Maximus; Baths of Caracalla; Tomb of the Scipios; Colum-
barin; Porta St. Sebastiano; Appian Way; Piazza Navona; Guard house of the
VII. Cohort; Churches of Santa Maria in Trastevere; St. Maria in Via Lata; St.
Maria Degl, Angeli; St. Pietro in Vinculi; Monte Cavallo and Quirinal; Baths of
Diocletian; Remains of the Agger of Servius Tullus; Church of St. Paul outside
the Walls; Walls and Gates of Rome; Painted Tombs on the Via Latina. Palaces:
—Quirinal, Doria, Colonna Orsini, Corsini, Spada, Barbarini, Farnese, Borghese.
Farnesina, &c., &c. Outside the walls excursions may be made to Ostia, Villa
Hadrian, Tivoli, Frascati, &c.

ROTTERDAM (Holland).—Pop. 129,000. Large commercial city. Places
of interest:—Cathedral, Old Church, South Church, Town Hall, Exchange, Botanical Gardens, Boyman's Museum, Groote, Market, &c.

STRASBURG (Alsace). Pop. 82,000. Taken from the French in 1870.
Places of interest:—Cathedral, one of the finest in the world, containing the
famous clock; statue of Gutenberg. The ascent of the Cathedral tower should be
made to obtain a view of the surrounding country.

TURIN (Italy).—Pop. 212,000. Places of interest:—Royal Palace, Churches
of St. John the Baptist, St. Filippe Neri and St. Lorenzo; University; Royal
Academy of Science; Academy of Arts, Egyptian Museum; Armory Museum;
Civic Museum; Palazzo Madanna, etc. The Church of Superga, 5 miles from
Turin, contains the Mausoleum of the Royal Family.

VENICE (Italy)--(pop. 129,000)-- is built on 72 islands, on piles, in the midst of a salt lagoon, or shallow lake. It is divided into two parts by the Grand Canal, the course of which flows through the city in the form of an inverted S, is 330 feet wide, crossed near the middle of its course by the Ponte di Rialto, a splendid marble structure of one spacious arch. In the midst of the labyrinth of canals and streets there are several large Piazzas, nearly all of which are adorned with fine churches or palaces. The principal of these is the Piazza di San Marco, a large oblong area 562 feet by 232, surrounded by elegant buildings, and containing at its extremity the Church of San Marco; a singular but brilliant combination of the Gothic and the Oriental style of architecture. In the Piazza is the Campanile, 316 feet high and 42 feet square, with a pyramidal top, to which the ascent is made by an inclined plane. Adjoining the Church are the ancient palace of the Doges, the prisons, and other public offices of the late Venetian Republic. San Marco was founded in the year 828, by the Doge Gnistiniano Participazio, for the purpose of receiving the relics of St. Mark. Principal places of interest:-- Cathedral, Churches of St. Maria della Salute, St. Giorgio Maggiore, Frari Scalzi, S. Salvatore, St. Sebastiano, St. Redentore, S. Rocco, S. Scuola, S. Pantaleone, S. Maria Carmine, S. Trovaso, S. Stefano, S. Zobenigo, S. Moise, S. Zanipolo, Jesuits, Madonna Dell Orto; Academy of Fine Arts; Doge's Palace; Royal Palace; Campanile; Armenian Convent on the Lido, etc.

VERONA (Italy).-- Pop. 60,000. Situated at the base of the Alps, on the river Adige. One of the most important fortified towns of northern Italy. Places of interest:--The Arena; Piazza del Signori; Palazza del Consiglio; Tombs of the Scalligeri; Cathedral, etc.

ZURICH (Switzerland).--Pop. 21,199. The capital of the Canton, situated on the north end of the Lake of Zurich, and on the banks of the river Limmat, and is one of the most flourishing manufacturing Swiss towns. Places of interest:- Town Library; Grossmunster; Cloisters; Town Hall, and Hohe Promenade.

☞*For a full description of the above places, the Traveler will do well to consult Cook's Tourist Guide Books, a list of which will be found on 2d page of cover of this pamphlet.*

NAMES OF A FEW OF THE DISTINGUISHED AMERICANS

WHO HAVE TRAVELED UNDER

THE ARRANGEMENTS OF THOS. COOK & SON.

Prof. Sam'l T. Ammen, Baltimore, Md.
Prof. B. D. Ames, Mechanicsville, N.Y.
Dr. W. E. Anthony, Providence, R. I.
Rev. Wm. P. Alcott, Hartford, Conn.
Prof. John J. Anderson, New York.
Rev. B. M. Adams, New Haven, Conn.
Dr. F. B. Ayer, Nassau, N. H.
Hon. T. T. Alexander, Louisville, Ky.
Rev. A. F. Beard, Syracuse, N. Y.
Prof. O. R. Burchard, Fredonia, N.Y.
Prof. O. B. Bruce, Binghamton, N. Y.
Rev. John H. Barrows, Springfield, Ill.
Wm. Ballantyne, Esq., Washington, D.C.
Dr. H. L. Bartholomew, Warren, Pa.
Rev. Jeremiah Butler, Fairport, N. Y.
Rev. Jno. S. Bayne, Portland, Conn.
Rev. Alfred A. Buttler, Cedar Rapids, Iowa.
Hon. Eugene D. Berri, Brooklyn, N. Y.
Lieut. Wm. H. Bixby, U. S. A.
Hon. B. K. Bruce, Mississippi.
Rev. E. Braslin, Mt. Holly, N. J.
Rev. J. H. Bayliss, Indianapolis, Ind.
Lieut. Geo. A. Bicknell, U. S. N.
Hon. Dan't. F. Beatty, Washington, N.J.
Rev. W. I. Budington, Brooklyn, N. Y.
Dr. Geo. W. Bird, Boston, Mass.
Rev. J. H. Bryson, Columbia, S. C.
Hon. John W. Bacon, Boston, Mass.
Hon. W. W. Blackmar, Boston, Mass.

Rev. W. F. Crafts, Boston, Mass.
Rev. Giles B. Cooke, Petersburg, Va.
Dr. Wm. Colton, E. Bethlehem, Pa.
Rev. E. N. Crane, Norfolk, Va.
Rev. Sam'l Colcord, New York.
Capt. I. M. Curtis, Washington, D. C.
Prof. Geo. F. Comfort, Syracuse, N. Y.
Prof. Narcisse Cyr, Boston, Mass.
Chas. Collyer, Esq., Chelsea, Mass.

Rev. Cyrus Dickson, D.D., New York.
Rev. C. F. Deems, D.D., New York.
Rev. Wm. H. De Puy, D. D., New York.

Prof. Joseph Daniels, Olivet, Mich.
Dr. J. H. Depuy, Wabash, Ind.
Prof. Chas. Drowne, Troy, N. Y.
Rev. R. Douglass, Louisville, Ky.

Prof. Irving Emerson, Hartford, Conn.

Rev. Edw'd W. French, Jersey City, N.J.
Dr. Geo. W. Fleming, Shelbyville, Ind.
W. J. A. Fuller, Esq., New York.
Prof. Geo. M. Furman, Binghamton, N.Y.
Prof. D. M. Fisk, Hillsdale, Mich.
Bishop R. S. Foster, Boston, Mass.
Prof. C. H. Fernald, Orono, Me.

Gen. U. S. Grant, Galena, Ill.
John B. Gough, Massachusetts.
Dr. John Green, St. Louis, Mo.
Rev. Emory Gale, St. Paul, Minn.
Hon. C. L. C. Gifford, Newark, N. J,
Prof. L. Greenwood, New York.
Hon. Henry A. Gumbleton, New York.
Rev. John F. Gorcher, Baltimore, Md.

Rev. Newman Hall, London.
Rev. E. O. Haven, D. D., LL. D., Syracuse, N. Y.
Prof. O. Howes, Hamilton, N. Y.
Rev. Geo. A. Hall, New York.
Rev. Theo. A. Hopkins, Burlington, Vt.
Rev. J. H. Hargis, Philadelphia, Pa.
Rev. Thos. Hanlon, D. D., Pennington, N. J.
Dr. C. M. Hoagland, Brooklyn, N. Y.
Rev. Chas. J. Hill, Ansonia, Conn.
Prof. J. H. Hoose, Cortland, N. Y.
Rev. F. B. Hodge, Wilkesbarre, Pa.
Rev. Andrew Hopper, Newark, N. J.
Prof. Chas. C. Hall, Glasgow, Mo.
Rev. T. W. Hooper, Lynchburg, Va.
Rev. J. E. L. Holmes, Danville, Va.
Rev. E. E. Higbee, D.D., Mercersburg, Pa.
Rev. James R. Hubbard, Winchester, Va.
Rev. J. P. D. John, Rushville, Ind.

Rev. H. M. Knox, St. Paul, Minn.
Rev. John Kilbourne, Buffalo, N. Y.
Rev. J. P. Knox, Newtown, L. I.
Joseph F. Knapp, Esq., Brooklyn, N. Y.
Rev. J. D. Knox, Topeka, Ks.
Prof. W. C. Kerr, Raleigh, N. C.
Rev. O. D. Kimball, Leominster, Mass.

Hon. W. I. Laval, Columbia, S. C.
Dr. N. C. Levings, New York.
Rev. M. B. Lowrie, Galesburg, Ill.
Henry Long, Esq., New York.

Rev. Sam'l B. Morse, Stockton, Cal.
Rev. Newland Maynard, Brooklyn, N.Y.
Dr. Thos. G. Morton, Philadelphia, Pa.
Rev. M. Meiggs, D. D., Pottstown, Pa.
Prof. R. H. Mather, Amherst, Mass.
Rev. G. D. Matthews, D. D., New York.
Rev.R.G. S. McNeille, Bridgeport,Conn.
Dr. P. F. Miesse, Chillicothe, O.
Hon. Sam'l W. Melton, Columbia, S. C.
S. T. G. Morsell, Esq.,Washington, D.C.
Capt. Louis Y. Mitchell, Washington, D. C.
Dr. W. A. Mitchell, Eufaula, Ala.
Col. H. C. Merriam, Brownsville, Texas.
Col. Benj. Mason, Yonkers, N. Y.
Dr. L. W. Munhall, Indianapolis, Ind.
Dr. G. L. Magruder, Washington, D. C.

Capt. R. Norwood, U. S. A.
Dr. R. J. Nunn, Savannah, Ga.
Dr. Geo. Nichols, Brooklyn, N. Y.
Dr. Frank Nichols, Hoboken, N. J.
Rev. H. E. Niles, D. D., York, Pa.
J. D. Nutter, Esq., Montreal, Can.

Hon. C. F. Olds, Cincinnati, O.
Rev. Fred. Oxnard, Sandwich, Mass.
Rev. Wm. Ormiston, D. D., New York.
Rev. J. S. Ostrander, New York.

Rev. F. Patton, D. D., Chicago, Ill.
Capt. Wm. Prince, U. S. A.
Rev. S. T. Pitts, Huntsville, Mo.
Rev. G. H. W. Petrie, D. D., Montgomery, Ala.
Prof. G. W. Plympton, Brooklyn, N. Y.
Rev. T. R. G. Peck, Yonkers, N. Y.

Dr. Chas. T. Parkes, Chicago, Ill.
Prof. Carlyle Pelersilea, Boston, Mass.
Ludlow Patton, Esq., New York.
S. B. Paige, Esq., Oshkosh, Wis.

Rev. Stuart Robinson, D. D., Louisville, Ky.
Rev. W. T. Richardson, Staunton, Va.
Rev. A. G. Ruliffson, New York.
Rev. Daniel Read, D.D., Brooklyn, N. Y.
Dr. J. B. Roberts, Sandersville, Ga.
Prof. A. L. Rawson, New York.
Prof. W. A. Reese, Westminster, Md.
Dr. J. C. Rosse, U. S. N.
Hon. Wm. B. Reed, Washington, D. C.
E. Russell, Esq., Boston, Mass.

Rev. Philip Schaff, D. D., New York.
Prof. James Strong, Madison, N. J.
Prof. John R. Sampson, Davidson College, N. C.
Rev. Jos. Stacy, Newman, Ga.
Hon. John T. Sloan, Columbia, S. C.
Dr. Edward Sutton Smith, New York.
Prof. B. J. Stone, New Milford, Conn.
Rev. P. A. Studdiford, D.D.,Trenton,N.J.
Prof. C. S. Stone, New York.
Dr. J. L. Sullivan, Malden, Mass.

Dr. J. M. Towler, Columbia, Tenn.
Rev. John B. Turpin, Richmond, Va.
Dr. Eben Tourjee, Boston, Mass.
Col. E. F. Townsend, U. S. A.
Daniel Torrance, Esq., New York.
Rev. W. P. Tilden, Boston, Mass.

Rev. J. G. Van Slyke, Kingston, N. Y.
Rev. T. E. Vassar, Flemington, N. J.
Chas. Viele, Esq., Evansville, Ind.

Prof. R. H. Willis, Jr., Nashville, Tenn.
Rev. T. D.Witherspoon, University of Va.
Hon. H. W. Williams, Wellsboro, Pa.
Dr. R. M. Whitefoot, Montana.
Rev. C. R. Ward, Plainfield, N. J.
Rev. Samuel Watson, Memphis, Tenn.
Leonard Waldo, Ph. D., Harvard College.
Rev. J. Zimmerman, Valatie, N. Y.
Prof. Carl Zerrahn, Boston, Mass.

NAMES OF A FEW OF THE FOREIGN NOTABILITIES,

WHO HAVE TRAVELED UNDER

THE ARRANGEMENTS OF THOS. COOK & SON.

Lady Ashburton.
Earl of Antrim.
Lord Arundel of Wardour.
Count C. E. S. D'Albanie.
Gen. Sir Jas. F. Alexander.
Major G. Abbot Anderson.
Sir Frederic and Lady Arrow
Rev. Dr. Allon.
Hon. George W. Allan.
Earl of Airlie.
Lord Ashley.

The Emperor and Empress of Brazil
  and suite.
Countess of Buchan.
Bishop of Bedford.
Lady Frederic Beauclerk.
Mrs. D'Arnaud-Bey (Cairo).
Terneau-Bey (Constantinople).
Chevalier De la Brunerie.
Baron Brusselli.
Professor Blackie.
Sir Redmond Barry.
Ven. Archdeacon Blunt.
Hon. Lady Brooke.
Major-Gen. Burrows.
Lord Boston.
Hon. and Rev. H. Bligh.
Gen. Blackford.
Lord Charles Bruce.
Bishop of Beverley.
Ven. Archdeacon Bailey.
Lady Beauchamp.
The Lord Chief Baron.
Admiral Blomfield.
Hon. and Rev. T. E. C. Byng.
Sir Reginald Barnewell.

His Grace Archbishop of Canterbury
  and Family.
Lord Chelmsford.
Dow. Lady Dick Cunyngham.
Lady Adelaide Cadogan.
The late Viscount Campden.
The Rt. Hon. W. Coghlan.
Hon. Alexander Campbell.
Admiral Coote.
Sir. Chas. Crossley.

Alderman Cotton (as Lord Mayor).
Colin Minton Campbell. Esq., M. P.
Bishop of Carlisle.
Baron Castagno.
Rev. Canon Connor.
Rt. Hon. Stephen Cave.
Sir G. Campbell.
Bishop of Cape Town.
Rev. Sir G. N. Cox.
Countess Cottenham.
Dean of Chester.
Rev. Canon Casenove.
Gen. Sir Arthur Cunynghame.
Dowager Viscountess Canterbury.
Sir Archibald Campbell.

The Countess Ducie.
Countess Dowager Donoughmore.
Earl of Denbigh
Lady Dunraven.
Rt. Rev. Bishop of Dover.
Viscount Dalrymple.
Lieut.-General Sir Percy Douglas.
Major-General M. C. Dixon.
General Sir C. Daubeny.
Hepworth Dixon, Esq.
Admiral Douglas.
Rev. Canon Drinkwater.
Lord Deas.
Hon. G. Duncan.
Rev. Canon Davys.
Bishop of Dunedin.
Earl and Countess of Dufferin and
  Family.

Lady Eastlake.
Marchioness of Ely.
The Hon. A. Erskine.
E. S. Ellis, Esq., J.P.
Bishop of Edinburgh.
Baron de la Tuille des Essarts.
Marquess of Ely.
Marquis and Marchioness of Exeter
  and Family.

Hon. A. N. Forbes.
Canon Fleming.
Dr. Clement Le Neve Foster.
Ven. Archdeacon Ffoulkes.

LADY AUGUSTUS FITZ CLARENCE.
SIGNOR FOLI.
GENERAL FEILDING.
EARL OF GAINSBOROUGH.
LADY LUCY GRANT.
LIEUT.-GEN. SIR JOHN ST. GEORGE.
ADMIRAL SIDNEY GRENFELL.
BISHOP OF GUILDFORD.
BISHOP OF GLOUCESTER AND BRISTOL.
RT. HON. W. E. GLADSTONE, M.P.
MRS. GLADSTONE AND FAMILY.
ARCHDEACON GRAY.
BARONESS DES GRANGES.
LADY CLAUDE HAMILTON.
SIR HENRY AND LADY HAVELOCK.
COUNT DU PONTIVEL DE HENSSEY.
BARON PAUL WASZ DE HOSTENSTEIN.
VICE-ADMIRAL SIR J. C. HAY.
REAR-ADMIRAL ROBERT HALL.
SIR B. F. HALL, BART.
MR. AND HON. MRS. KING HARMAN.
DOWAGER LADY HATHERTON.
DOWAGER MARCHIONESS OF HUNTLEY.
VEN. ARCHDEACON HUNTER.
LORD HILTON.
VISCOUNT HARBERTON.
ADMIRAL SIR PHIPPS HORNBY.
SIR ARTHUR HOBHOUSE.
REV. LORD CHARLES HERVEY.
CANON HAMILTON.
SIR HENRY HOLLAND.
MAJOR-GEN. CHAS. IRVINE.
COL. AND HON. MRS. IVES.
LADY CAROLINE KERRISON.
HON. ARTHUR KINNAIRD.
DEAN OF KILMORE.
LADY ANNA LOFTUS.
EARL OF LIMERICK.
LORD ALEX. GORDON LENNOX.
GEN. R. C. LAWRENCE.
LORD LENNOX.
BISHOP OF LICHFIELD.
REV. CANON LONSDALE.
REV. CANON LEIGHTON.
LADY JANE LEVETT.
PRINCE LUBOMORSKI.
GENERAL LORING.
DOWR. COUNTESS OF LONSDALE.
COUNTESS MARSOENSHOEWSNOFF.
COUNTESS MAYO.
LORD ROBT. MONTAGUE, M. P.
ADMIRAL MILLER.
COUNT METTERNICH.
GEN. COLIN MACKENZIE.
SIR JAS. MALCOLM.
SIR G. MONTGOMERY, M. P.
SIR C. R. MCGREGOR, BART.
SIR R. AND LADY MUSGRAVE.

SAMUEL MORLEY, ESQ., M. P.
ARCHDEACON MATHIAS.
MAJOR-GEN. MOULD.
VISCOUNT MALDEN.
HON. V. MONTAGUE.
GENERAL S. F. MACMULLEN.
BISHOP MCDOUGALL.
LT.-COL. W. G. MONTGOMERY.
ALDERMAN MCARTHUR, M. P.
EARL OF MULGRAVE.
MAJOR-GENERAL MACINTYRE.
DUKE OF NORFOLK.
MAJOR-GENERAL H. NOTT.
HON. RICHARD NUGENT.
REV. CANON NISBET.
SIR P. CUNLIFFE OWEN.
LORD ORANMORE.
LORD AND LADY ALFRED PAGET.
SIR GEO. BROOKE PECHELL.
COL. SIR RICHARD POLLOCK.
REV. MORLEY PUNSHON.
SAMUEL PLIMSOLL, ESQ., M. P.
SIR ROBERT PEEL.
RIGHT REV. BISHOP PERRY.
VEN. ARCHDEACON POTT.
LORD RADSTOCK.
SIR WM. ROSE, K. C. B.
BARON RASSLER.
REV. DR. ROBERTSON.
REV. CANON RICKARDS.
ADMIRAL ROSS.
MRS. JOHN WATTS RUSSELL.
EARL OF SHREWSBURY.
SIR JAMES KAY SHUTTLEWORTH.
SIR JOHN AND LADY SEBRIGHT.
VISCOUNTESS STRANGFORD.
SIR FRANCIS SANDFORD, C. B.
ADMIRAL SELWYN.
LIEUT-COL. HENRY SHAKESPEARE.
MR. C. H. SPURGEON.
COUNT DE LA SALLE.
GEN. SHIPLEY.
MISS STANLEY (The Deanery, Westminster).
VERY REV. DEAN SPOONER.
COUNT SECKENDORF.
LADY TEMPLE.
COL. THE HON. WM. TALBOT.
HON. AND REV. EDWARD S. TALBOT.
LORD DE TABLEY.
LORD VERNON.
LADY WINGATE.
SIR JOHN WALROND, BART.
MAJOR-GEN. SIR GARNET WOLSELEY, K. C. B.
CANON WADE.
LORD WESTBURY.
LADY FOX YOUNG.

www.ingramcontent.com/pod-product-compliance
Lightning Source LLC
Chambersburg PA
CBHW032043090426
42733CB00030B/642